When a spiritual book that is more than fifty years old is still full of profound and challenging spiritual insights, it tells us very much about the deep faith and wisdom of the author. Clarence Enzler's work has touched many lives and brought many people closer to the Lord. It still has the power to do that; it is still a book to be read with reflection and profit today.

Cardinal Theodore E. McCarrick
Archbishop Emeritus of Washington

Ave Maria Press has done all of us a great service by bringing back into print Clarence Enzler's *My Other Self.* It is a rich vein of lived spirituality that reflects a life of growing into Christ. Each page, whether reflecting on the call to oneness with Christ, the means by which we achieve this end or the final goal itself, offers the reader penetrating insight, uncompromising challenge, and gentle encouragement. Written from the heart, it has the power to touch the heart. I enthusiastically recommend *My Other Self* as a companion on life's journey with Christ.

Most Rev. Donald W. Wuerl
Archbishop of Washington

Clarence Enzler's classic speaks a language of devotion and faith that is ever new. Read it and live a change of heart—an entry into the life of Christ and the fulfillment of the life you most hunger to live.

Timothy P. Shriver
President
Special Olympics

Modeled on the fifteenth-century classic, *The Imitation of Christ*, *My Other Self* presents Christ speaking intimately to the heart of his disciple. Deeply biblical and rooted in the tradition of the Church, the book is a practical guide for Christians living in the contemporary world. Like the original, it would make a wonderful companion for prayer.

Thomas P. Rausch, S.J.
T. Marie Chilton Professor of Catholic Theology
Loyola Marymount University

My Other Self offers readers a sanctuary from today's frantic and complicated world. Not only does it help us comprehend the depths of Jesus' love for us, the way in which it is written also humanizes him. I became so enraptured by the dialogue that I actually felt like Jesus was having a conversation with me, almost as if I was talking to a peer. This is a timeless classic that will undoubtedly help you develop and maintain a relationship with Christ.

Guiomar Ochoa
International Activities Specialist
National Endowment for the Arts

My Other Self is an ideal guide for young Christians striving to live a devout life in today's world. Enzler's approach is deceptively simple. By showing over and over again "the eternal now" of Christ, he reveals the true path to happiness—which can seem remote and abstract beside the temptations of today's world—to be the most intimate, real, and desirable path imaginable. Whether already a practicing, orthodox Catholic, or hoping to become one, any young person will be enlightened and delighted by this brilliant work.

Mela Kirkpatrick
Johns Hopkins University

MY OTHER SELF

CONVERSATIONS WITH CHRIST
ON LIVING YOUR FAITH

Clarence J. Enzler

Foreword by Benedict Groeschel, C.F.R.

Christian Classics ⌘ *Notre Dame, Indiana*

Nihil Obstat:

Joannes A. Schulien, S.T.D.
Censor Librorum

Imprimatur:

† Albertus G. Meyer
Archiepiscopus Milwauchiensis
October 8, 1957

Except as otherwise noted, all New Testament citations are from *The New Testament* as translated by James A. Kleist, S.J., and Joseph L. Lilly, C.M. (Milwaukee: The Bruce Publishing Company, 1956).

First published 1957 as *My Other Self: In Which Christ Speaks to the Soul on Living HIS Life.*

Founded in 1865, Ave Maria Press is a ministry of the Indiana Province of Holy Cross.

www.christian-classics.com

ISBN-10 0-87061-248-4 ISBN-13 978-0-87061-248-0

Cover image Jesus the Comforter by August Andreas Jerndorf (1846-1906) © Superstock.

Cover design by John R. Carson.

Text design by Katherine Robinson Coleman.

Printed and bound in the United States of America.

Library of Congress Cataloging-in-Publication Data

Enzler, Clarence J.
   My other self : conversations with Christ on living your faith / Clarence J. Enzler ; foreword by Benedict Groeschel.
       p. cm.
   Originally published: 1957. With new introductory matter.
   Includes bibliographical references (p.   ).
   ISBN-13: 978-0-87061-248-0 (pbk.)
   ISBN-10: 0-87061-248-4 (pbk.)
   1.   Spirituality--Catholic Church. 2.   Spiritual life--Catholic Church. 3. Christian life--Catholic authors.   I. Title.
   BX2350.65.E59 2010
   248.4'82--dc22

2010035954

CLARENCE JOSEPH ENZLER (1910–1976) is best known for his classic Lenten devotional booklet *Everyone's Way of the Cross*, first published in 1970. He worked for the US Department of Agriculture from 1937–1972, except from 1943–1945 when he served as the feature editor with the National Catholic Welfare Conference News Service (now known as Catholic News Service).

O, all-powerful, all-wise, all-loving TRINITY, to whose honor and glory this work is dedicated, grant that it may come into the hands of those who, because they wish to love you more, will use it profitably.

Instruct them—every one—in how they may use it most wisely in order to serve you better and love you more.

CONTENTS

FOREWORD

I am very pleased that after far too many years of being out of print, Clarence Enzler's fine book, *My Other Self,* is being republished by Ave Maria Press. This little book has meant a great deal to many people in the past and I am sure that in its new edition it will soon become very meaningful to a whole new generation of Catholics and other Christians.

Written by a layman and father of thirteen children who eventually was ordained to the diaconate, *My Other Self* is a deeply devotional book. It is also a beautiful book and one that is very accessible to most Catholics. Composed of a series of meditations (or, perhaps more properly, soliloquies) in which Christ speaks directly to the individual human soul, this book reminds us over and over again of the infinite gentleness and love that our Divine Savior has for us. Here we find hardly a trace of the wrath of God or even of a stern God. Instead we find Christ as our compassionate teacher, as the gentle but endlessly fervent lover of our souls. Enzler reminds us again and again of what, in our difficult world, we can often forget: Christ cares for us so deeply that he will never give up on us, that his divine will is that we spend eternity in endless joyful relationship with him.

Enzler shows us that the life of the Christian is really a life of trust—trust in Christ, who gave himself for us and will never stop loving us. In fact, it seems to me that "trust" is really the key to this book, a trust in Christ that is so great that it eventually enables us to allow all the impediments to a full relationship with God to fall away. Trust in our world is difficult, but Enzler is very aware that we become able to trust by responding to the endless outpouring of tender love that Christ offers us, even in our most difficult moments. Even our tragedies and failures become occasions of trust, because we come to understand them as a mysterious part of the love that Christ continually offers us. When we respond to this love and begin to trust, we enter into the extraordinarily intimate relationship with Christ that Enzler sees as the goal of the Christian life. The title, *My Other Self*, of course, refers to this. It is Christ's ultimate purpose to turn us into images of him. By trusting in Christ and lovingly living the life he has ordained for us we become able to accept the ultimate gift from him. We become his mirrors. As he looks at us he sees himself, and so we enter into union with him.

Those who are familiar with Catholic devotional literature will be immediately aware that *My Other Self* stands directly in the tradition of that great classic, *The Imitation of Christ*. In fact, I have no doubt that the earlier book was Enzler's inspiration. However, I see in *My Other Self* not just connections to *The Imitation of Christ*, but to other areas of Catholic thought and devotion. At times Enzler's book makes one think of the "little way" of Saint Thérèse. He speaks repeatedly of the need to imitate Christ in the circumstances in which Christ has placed us, to make holy the ordinary things of life, not to strive after great things but to find the greatness Christ offers us in the little things of our lives. *My Other Self* could easily be tied to the Divine Mercy (a devotion of which Enzler may not even have been aware back in the fifties when he wrote his book). On the picture of the Divine Mercy which now hangs in every Catholic Church there are the words "Jesus, I trust in you." Enzler's book beautifully reminds us of why we should and must trust Christ, and it shows us that Christ is always eager to give us ways in which we can enter into his eternal embrace.

In a world that seems in danger of losing a sense of God or at least of imagining God as very distant or even impersonal, a book like this one can become very important. I urge all Catholics to read it slowly and meditatively—perhaps even one short chapter a day. I assure you the time will be well spent and the reward considerable.

Father Benedict J. Groeschel, C.F.R.

Biographical Introduction

We write this reflection about our dad from the perspective of being born into a close-knit Catholic family under the guidance of unparalleled parents, Kathleen Crowley Enzler and Clarence J. Enzler. They were married in Washington, DC, in 1937. Mom was a native Washingtonian; Dad, who grew up in Dubuque, Iowa, attended Columbia College and received his doctorate in sociology from Catholic University in the mid-1930s.

Our dad grew up with a speech impediment, a debilitating stutter that kept him from public speaking for many years. He eventually became an excellent speaker and International Toast Master contestant. Seemingly, his impediment spurred him on to develop excellent writing skills. He spent thirty-two years as an Information Specialist/Speechwriter for the Secretary of Agriculture. He was ordained a deacon for the Archdiocese of Washington in 1972 and served at St. Mary, Mother of God Catholic Church in the heart of Washington until his untimely death in 1976.

Those are the facts. What these details do not describe is a fabulous father who had great gifts of compassion, love, and care for each of his children. All

xiv

thirteen of us remember him fondly for the way his guidance and support taught us the value and joy of living in Jesus' image every day.

The best times for our family were when we were together celebrating evening meals and special holidays, particularly Christmas. We would gather around on Christmas Eve, opening presents and sharing fun. My father had a favorite quote that is still remembered by all of us who enjoyed his infectious spirit. He would look around and simply say, "Isn't this fun!" That's a memory we all have of our father and our mom and our life growing up in the '40s, '50s and '60s just outside of Washington. Life was fun. Yes, there was faith. We laughed and enjoyed so many special times together, but our belief in God and his presence in our lives were always paramount in all we did. Those gifts came from our dad and mom, and they are celebrated in a special way in his reflections and words of *My Other Self*.

How does a man work overtime for the government; write four books, numerous articles, and a devotional Stations of the Cross; be involved as a leader in his parish (particularly as a member of the St. Vincent de Paul Society, where he visited and took care of the elderly and poor); yet make time to attend Mass every day and spend quality time with each of his thirteen children during each stage of our lives? His legacy is strong and powerful as a deacon here in Washington, as a dedicated civil servant and as a man of kindness and love for all. His real legacy was his devotion to our mom during their thirty-nine-year marriage and his absolute, unconditional love for each of his children.

Dad lived the words of *My Other Self* and he lived them well. He was a model Christian, an outstanding Catholic, a defender of the faith, a gifted and skilled writer, a fabulous husband and an unparalleled father. But most of all, he was a man of God. The word you are about to read speak of his faith, his union with the Lord and his love for Jesus. Enjoy the spiritual reflections and come to know how one man endeavored to be Christ's other self.

The Enzler Family:
Jean, Carol, Mary Pat, Marge,
Kathy, John, Connie, Jim, Jerry,
David, Eileen, Tom, and Brenda

PREFACE

Since the style of this book is somewhat unusual, a few remarks concerning its structure may be helpful. I have, to a great extent, adapted the mode of presentation followed by the author of the *Imitation of Christ.* Thus, the reader will find Christ speaking to him in intimate conversations, seeking to make him fully aware of what it means to be a Christian, "another Christ," Christ's "other self."

My aim has been to unfold, as fully as I can, the meaning of union with our Lord and all that it involves both for the individual and for society. I have sought to show that the *present* moment is Christ's moment, the time for each individual to identify himself with the Lord and to act as Christ. If this book realizes this goal, even to the slightest degree, it will have fulfilled my purpose.

Clarence J. Enzler

THE PRIESTLY PRAYER OF JESUS CHRIST

Father, the hour is come!
Glorify your Son,
that your Son may glorify you.
You have given him authority over all mankind
that he might give eternal life to all you have
entrusted to him.
And this is the sum of eternal life—
their knowing you, the only true God, and your
ambassador Jesus Christ.

I have glorified you on earth
by completing the work you gave me to do.
And now, for your part, Father,
glorify me in your bosom,
with the glory I possessed in your bosom
before the world existed.

I have made your name known to the men
whom you singled out from the world
and entrusted to me.
Yours they were,
and to me you have entrusted them;

and they cherish your message.
Now they know
that whatever you have given me
really comes from you;
for the message you have delivered to me
I have delivered to them;
and they have accepted it.

They really understand
that I come from you,
and they believe that I am your ambassador.
I am offering a prayer for them;
not for the world do I pray,
but for those whom you have entrusted to me;
for yours they are.
All that is mine is yours,
and yours is mine;
and they are my crowning glory.

I am not long for this world;
but they remain in the world,
while I am about to return to you.
Holy Father!
Keep them loyal to your name
which you have given me.
May they be one as we are one! . . .

I have delivered to them your message;
and the world hates them,
because they do not belong to the world,
just as I do not.

I do not pray you
to take them out of the world,
but only to preserve them from its evil influence.
The world finds nothing kin in them,
just as the world finds nothing kin in me.
Consecrate them to the service of truth.
Your message is truth.

As you have made me your ambassador to the
    world,
so I am making them my ambassadors to the
    world;
and for their sake I consecrate myself,
that they, in turn, may in reality be consecrated.

However, I do not pray for them alone;
I also pray for those
who through their preaching will believe in me.

All are to be one;
just as you, Father, are in me and I am in you,
so they, too, are to be one in us.
The world must come to believe
that I am your ambassador.

The glory you have bestowed on me
I have bestowed on them,
that they may be one as we are one,
—I in them and you in me.
Thus their oneness will be perfected.
The world must come to acknowledge

that I am your ambassador,
and that you love them as you love me.

O Father!
I will that those whom you have entrusted to me
shall be at my side.
I want them to behold my glory,
the glory you bestowed on me
because you loved me
before the world was founded.

Just Father!
The world does not know you,
but I know you,
and thus these men have come to know
that I am your ambassador.
I have made known to them your name,
and I will continue to make it known.
May the love which you love me
dwell in them
as I dwell in them myself.[1]

PART I

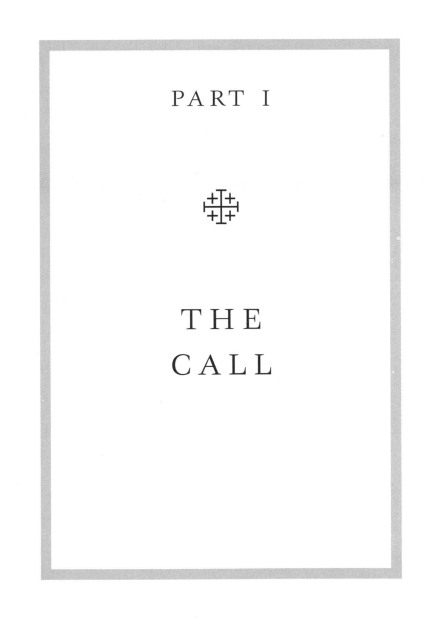

THE
CALL

chapter one

THE GOAL OF LIFE

In Christ's Presence

> O Lord, our Lord, how wonderful is thy name
> in all the earth.
>
> Psalm 8:2

My dear friend, I am overjoyed to see you. I am with you speaking to you and listening to you. Realize that I am truly present. I am within your soul. Close your ears and eyes to all distractions. Retire within yourself, think my thoughts, and be with me alone.

Do not be afraid. I am your God, your King, robed in majesty, clothed with all power. But I am also human, even as you. I am your Savior.

Do you note what I call you? My friend. Not my creature, not my servant, but my friend. Yes, even more than that, you are my brother, my sister, my mother. Whoever does the will of my Father in heaven is my brother, my sister, my mother.

I am glad that you desire to watch a while with me, to confide in me and allow me to confide in you.

Have you ever wondered what I would have said to you if you had been at my side as Peter was, and John, Mary, Martha, and the rest?

Do you feel that they were especially favored to have lived when they did, because they saw me, heard me, touched me?

Yes; they were favored. But so are you. It is better for you to live now than at any other time in human history.

Do you not realize that this is my hour just as much as nineteen centuries ago? I see you just as clearly as I saw them. I love you as I loved them. I speak to you. Your good impulses, what are they but my grace and the urgings of the Holy Spirit?

But still you are thinking: They saw you face to face.

What was it that my disciples saw? They saw a man; a worker of wonders, yes, but only a man. It was many months before they knew me as "He who is to come," the messias; and as "He Who Is," God. And when they knew me at last, it was not by the sight of their eyes but by faith. It could not be otherwise. No mortal can see God face to face and live on in this world.

That is exactly how you know me today: by faith.

Happy, then, are you, happy and thrice blessed. Blessed are you because you see me with surer eyes than those of your human nature: the eyes of faith.

Blessed are you because you speak with me in words more easily understood than those of your mouth: prayer of the heart.

Yes, blessed are you, my friend, because you can more easily become intimately associated with me than could my closest followers before the Last Supper.

Peter and Andrew, James and John; and even my own Mother, for many years of their lives did not enjoy the wondrous privilege that awaits you every day. Never during those many months before the Supper did I unite myself with them so closely as I am united with you in Holy Communion. Already you have had more moments of intimate union with me in my sacrament than some of my dearest disciples had in their whole lives.

If you but let me I will come to you daily in the Sacrament of Love. I will come as man. And I will come as God, bringing the Trinity most intimately into your soul. I do not stay away from you; it is you who stay away from me.

Adam and Eve wished to be as God, and could not. But you, despite all your unworthiness, can become "as God" daily in Holy Communion. I enter into you, live in you, transform you. And when my Father looks on you, he sees you no longer, but me, his only-begotten Son.

Indeed you are especially favored, far more than you can realize. Think how many there are in the world who do not even know my Name! Why are you so blessed and not these others?

Why is it my will that you should be so intimate with me? Why have I destined you from eternity for this happy hour with me? Why have I sought you, called you, urged you, aided you all the days of your life to bring you close to me?

It is because my love for you passes human understanding.

Do you wonder how you shall thank your God? Thank me by making your soul a true home for me, and from that home offering myself and yourself in divine thanksgiving to the Holy and Undivided Trinity.

Think of this now. Think of it often. Think of it calmly, peacefully, and give me your heart, your mind, your will.

Say to my Father, "I thank you, Lord, with all of myself. I will contemplate all your wondrous deeds. I will be glad and rejoice, and I will sing praise to your holy Name."[1]

Christ, the Teacher of Happiness

> Happy are the blameless, who walk in the way
> of the Lord.
>
> PSALM 118:1

My dear friend, my greatest desire is that you be happy. It would be more impossible for me not to want you to be happy than for you not to want to eat when you are hungry.

I am not good merely as a creature is good. I am goodness. Goodness is of my very nature. You cannot fully comprehend that. I ask only that you believe it.

Believe that I am goodness itself. Believe that I want your happiness far more than you yourself want it. Believe that I can and will give you happiness.

I have made you in my own image, able to share in my divine life, and destined for that life. Give me your good will here on earth, and your happiness even in this life will surpass your dreams. And when you reach your eternal destiny, your joy will be such as you could never begin to imagine.

Do not refuse to do what will make you happy. Millions of your fellow men spurn me. Adam and Eve, anxious to do as they pleased, lost Paradise.

The chosen people of old, instructed by the prophets and even by my Father himself, refused to walk in his ways. They murdered the prophets. They worshiped idols and false gods. They gave themselves up to lust in the wilderness. And the wrath of the Lord was so kindled against them that he delivered them into the hands of nations who oppressed and humbled them.

I came upon the earth, sharing in your lowly manhood. By my own life I have shown you how to be happy.

Although I constantly teach men peace and contentment through my Church, many close their ears. They seek joy in a thousand vanities and ten thousand pleasures. But the happiness they pursue in sin turns to ashes in their mouths.

Listen to me. Turn to me, give me your mind, your heart, your soul. I shall not hide the truth from you. You desire happiness. I shall teach you the ways of happiness.

Happy is the one who does not follow the advice of the wicked, who does not walk in sin, who does not insult his Maker by foolish pride.

Happy is he who is considerate of the needy and the poor.

Happy are the blameless who follow in my path, who keep my laws night and day, who seek me with their whole heart.

Happy are all who take refuge in me. I shall be their shield, encouraging them and protecting them against danger. They will not fear any evil, even though thousands of enemies are arrayed against them on every side.

They will have great peace. For them there is no stumbling block.

I say to you, happy shall you be if you fear your Lord and walk trustingly in his way.

Yes, I will your happiness. Never believe that I desire anything but peace and contentment for you. I have given you my own happiness, my own joy, my very own peace. I want you to be a peacemaker, a maker of joy and happiness for those about you. I have commissioned you to help reconcile the world with me, to bring my peace to earth.

I desire your love, and the product of love is not depression, but happiness, enthusiasm, joy. What have you to fear? Live joyfully! Live happily! Live enthusiastically! Your joy is that God exists, ruling all, caring for all.

You will not draw to me the souls I long for so greatly by being ill-natured, gloomy, a pessimist.

Did I not say, "When you fast, do not imitate the gloomy looking hypocrites"?[2]

And did I not say, "Come to me . . . and I will refresh you"?[3]

It grieves me that so many believe that I am a stern, hard God, pleased by the spectacle of lowly man wiping the sweating brow of his soul while he asks himself, "Can I be saved? Can I possibly be saved?"

Did I give my life for you to torment you? To cause you anxiety?

I do not dwell in gloom, darkness, or dejection, but in light, love, and joy. Be of good heart.

Even when men revile you and persecute you and speak all manner of evil against you falsely because of me, be glad and lighthearted.

I am your light and your salvation. Whom shall you fear?

I am the defense of your life. Whom shall you dread?

With a great desire, I desire your happiness. I can make you happy. I will make you happy.

Be lighthearted, then, and rejoice in me that you may dwell in my house all the days of your life and enjoy my graciousness and kindness.

Christ, Maker of Saints

> Rejoice in the fact that your names are
> engraved in heaven.
>
> LUKE 10:20

My friend, the secret of happiness, here on earth and hereafter, is to be as saintly as possible. A saint is a person who is happy—forever.

To be a saint is one goal that you surely can reach. To be healthy, rich, honored, may be beyond your power. But you can confidently expect to be a saint. Ask this of me, and you shall receive it.

Trust yourself to me without reserve; and I say to you that it will be far easier for you to become a saint than not to become one.

You desire happiness. Happiness lies in holiness.

Do not think that holiness consists of unremitting penance, of hair shirts and bloody scourgings, of trances and ecstasies, of long nights spent motionless in prayer.

These are not essential to holiness. Holiness consists of but one thing: the union of your will with mine.

The one service you have in your power to give me is to do my will. The act of love that most honors me is to make your will one with mine, to desire nothing except what I desire, to will all that I will.

It is not sacrifice, but love, that melts my heart.

I shall show you how to be a saint. Do as I did; follow in my footsteps.

I became man not to do my will, but the will of him who sent me. I exalted my Father's glory on earth by doing the task he set before me. I became man at the precise moment and in the exact place he willed me to do so.

In the same way, I have appointed you a task: to bear fruit, to be my witness. For this reason you live at this time, in this nation, in this community, under these particular circumstances. Had you the wisdom of all the angels, you could not have chosen a better time and place for your life. You live here because it is best for you.

Follow me. You will bear abundant fruit if you live in me and I in you; separated from me, you can do nothing. Unite your will with mine, for that union is perfection, holiness, sanctity. In sanctity lies your happiness.

I do not expect you to become perfect overnight. Yet, if I so desire, I can make you perfect in a single instant. In my sight time is nothing; one day is a thousand years.

Be not impatient. Let me mold you as I choose. Let me form in you the image of myself. Let me transform you into me.

Let me teach you, in my own way, the ABCs of sanctity.

Some souls, touched by my consolations, seek to run too fast. They strive almost to kill themselves by penances and fasting. They wish to take on more than they can bear. Avaricious for spiritual advancement, they are forever comparing what they do with the "little" that others do. They want to pray longer than anyone else, to wield greater influence with me, to convert more souls than my great saints. They advance a little in holiness and they fancy themselves perfect. They impede their progress, they sometimes even retrogress, because they refuse to allow me to mold them in my own way.

Be different, I beg you.

Do not let spiritual pride take root in you. Do not be jealous of those who seem more "favored." Be patient. Give me your whole self to do with as I please, in all things, every day of your life, and I promise to shower grace upon you. I shall lead you to a firm, true, unselfish love. I shall remove from you the desire for consolation, and make you content with whatever I send. You will do penance for love of me, but you will learn that penance of itself is a little thing. Millions of persons throughout the world live daily lives of far greater deprivation than you with all your penances, because millions are always hungry, insecure, sick, cold, frightened, lonely. You will understand that holiness does not consist in penance and sacrifice, but in union with my will.

You will realize that I do not wish you to pray when your present duty calls you to active work, and that I do not will that you should work when it is time for prayer.

You will learn that of yourself you are nothing.

Everything good that you do or think comes from me.

Your soul, my dear friend, is but the instrument upon which I work. It is the reservoir into which the water of grace flows. All that you can do is to open or close its valve by the action of your will.

Although your achievements for me may be negligible, the gift of yourself is priceless in my eyes.

Your one desire will be that I may be served and loved. No longer will you desire to be my personal instrument for conversions, for preaching, for wonder-working. No longer will you desire to do more than anyone else. You will only want more to be done. And you will gladly be the least in my Father's house, if by being the least my glory is better served.

You will put on my virtues. You will be a victim with me for the salvation of mankind. You will be another Christ. Identified with me, you will be my other self.

That is the union with me that the greatest saints achieved.

That is the union with me that I have destined for you.

chapter two

ABANDONMENT

Confidence in Christ

> In thee, O my God, I put my trust.
>
> PSALM 24:2

I shall teach you the ABCs of holiness.

If you would be holy, surrender yourself to me. Trust me. Abandon yourself to me completely, without reserve, grasping eagerly whatever I send you, pleasant or bitter. It is my gift to you, part of my plan for your happiness. It is not merely good; you have only to make proper use of it and it is best.

Try to realize that I see all your thoughts and emotions, all your troubles and desires. I know you far more intimately than you know yourself. I know you not only as you are, but as you have been, and as you will be; and I know all of this NOW. There is no past or future with me; there is only the eternal now.

Do you find it hard to realize these truths? Can you comprehend how I can be intimately interested in you along with billions of men, women, and children, past, present, and future?

It is not necessary for you to comprehend. Only believe.

I look on you not only with intimate knowledge but with limitless love. That should touch you keenly: my love for my creatures, for you as an individual. How can you deny me your love?

I am near you, beholding you, guiding you, protecting you. I am within you. I am, in a sense, nearer to you than you are to yourself.

Why then do you not trust me? Do you not realize my power? I made you out of nothing. Having made you out of nothing, I hold you in existence, re-creating you every instant. You exist by a continuing act of my creative love. If at any moment I should withdraw my will, you would again become nothing. You would simply cease, utterly. This is true of all things: the earth, the sun and moon, the whole universe. It is true of all created beings: angels, devils, saints, sinners, even my own human nature.

If, then, I hold you and all things in existence by my will, not one thing can happen without my permission.

The sun cannot shine, the earth turn, a bird sing, a seed grow, the lightning strike, a stone be dislodged, unless I allow it. No man can harm you, no breath of wind disturb a hair of your head.

You cannot move, talk, listen, feel, see, or think without my concurrence. You have life from me, and I must sustain that life at every instant or it will fail. You have strength from me, and I must renew it at every instant or it will be nothing.

Of yourself you cannot raise your finger, blink your eye; your heart cannot beat, your lungs expand. You cannot think a single thought without my doing much more of the work than you do yourself. I have a far greater part in your actions than does the parent who guides a baby in its first steps or leads his little son's hand as he draws with a pencil.

Even your will is my gift to you, and I influence it at every moment by my grace.

Literally you can do nothing, neither good nor evil, without me. I am in all that you do; all that you do, you can do only in, with, and through my power.

When you sin, in a sense you force me to cooperate in the physical aspect of your offense, because your freedom and strength are from me.

Have confidence in me. You know that God is goodness, but you must meditate more on this attribute of mine. I am goodness without limit; there is no evil in me. I can do no evil. I can will no evil. Whatever I will must be not only good but best in every way. I cannot even permit evil, except for a greater good. Since all my acts flow from infinite goodness and infinite power, all that I do is equally perfect, equally good.

Whatever I do is perfect. Whatever I send you or permit to happen to you is, under the circumstances, the best that could be. You may not recognize my will at this particular moment as perfect; just as a child may fail to see the wisdom of a surgeon who is trying to save its life by applying perfect medical treatment.

Yet, for those who love me, all things work together for good. They must. I will have it no other way.

This is my power. Realize it. Ponder it. Meditate, and understand how foolhardy it is not to trust in me. How foolish to resist my will, when no one can alter my decrees. I am your refuge and your strength. Abandon yourself to me.

Motives for Trust

> I have loved you with an everlasting love.
>   JEREMIAH 31:3

Do not doubt me, my friend. Do not be irritated at your pain, your losses, your sickness, your enemies. View them as the means by which I guide you to myself. A wise parent does not forbid the child ever to run for fear it may fall or ever to leave the yard for fear it may be lost. The parent acts thus in love, and I act in much more perfect love. If opposition and affliction were not the food of your spiritual growth, I would never allow them to approach you, much less touch you. I send you nothing that is too heavy for you to bear. Everything is fitted precisely to your strength.

If you realized my love for you, you would surely have confidence in me. Before the world was made, I loved you. When there was no earth, no sun, no angels, I knew you were to be, when you would appear, what place you would have in my plan, how long you would live, what thoughts you would think and what prayers you would pray—and I loved you. Time never was when I did not love you. My making you was the expression of my infinite, eternal love, as the kiss you bestow is the expression of your finite love.

Since I am all-powerful, all-good, and since I love you far more than you love yourself, do not be afraid to abandon yourself wholly to me. I will teach you all that you must know and help you with all that you must do.

Is there anything that I have not done, and that I can do, to win your complete confidence? Tell me and I will do it. Remember, I died for you.

Abandon your will to mine, and all that happens must speed you along the path to happiness, to holiness, to sainthood. Under my loving care, nothing can harm you. Whatever happens to you by my will is so good that the angels of heaven themselves could not conceive of anything better.

Cling to me with all your heart, with all your will, and I will make you a saint. Nothing shall separate you from my love: neither death nor life, angels nor devils, neither things present nor to come. No force or creature in heaven or hell can separate my love from you if you do my will.

Trust in me; I will always protect you. Seek my will in all things. Your greatest good is that my will shall be done.

If you generously renounce your own will to seek only my good pleasure, my divine Heart will illumine you with a vivid light to know my wishes. I will show you what you must do and work within you to help you to accomplish it. I will let you lean on my Heart.

Pray to me, then, not that your will may be done, but that mine may be done in you. If I offered you joy in one hand and sorrow in the other, do you know what I would wish you to say to me? "Lord, I choose neither. Whichever is your will, let that be done." And since you would abandon your own will entirely to mine, I would pour into you all the sweetness and joy of my divine Heart.

This is my pledge, my word that endures forever, firm as heaven.

Trust me! Give me your entire self—your body and all its activities.

Trust me! Give me your soul and all its faculties.

Trust me! Give all that you possess, all that you are and will be, all that you do and will do.

Trust me! Give yourself to me without thought of reward, as I have given myself to the Father.

Trust me! Give me yourself continually and forever. Frequently renew your abandonment to my will. Renew it in the morning when you awake—when you receive me in Holy Communion—when you are at your meals—when you are at leisure—when you go to sleep—and renew it especially before all your principal actions and in the midst of trials.

Trust me! Say to me, as in the Psalms of David, "In God, whose promise I praise, in God I put my trust, I will not fear; what can man do to me"[1]; "O my strength, to thee will I sing praise, for thou, O God, art my defense; my God, my mercy."[2]

And I, in turn, will say to you as to my disciples, "Do not let your heart be troubled! . . . If you ask me for anything in my name, I will do it. . . . I will not leave you orphans. . . . Peace is my legacy to you: my own peace is my gift to you . . . Just as the Father loves me, so I love you."[3]

Spiritual Childhood

> The Lord is the keeper of the little ones.
>
> PSALM 114:6

The life of trust that I wish you to lead is the peaceful, sweet, serene life of a child in the arms of its parent—a life free from fear, from worry and care, and in a sense free from desire.

Let your soul be as David's when he sang: "As a little child on its mother's lap: as a little child, so is . . . my soul within me . . . hope in the Lord, both now and forever."[4]

What mother looking lovingly upon the infant on her lap could wish it evil? Yet the love of a mother, even the love of my Mother for me, is nothing to my love for you.

I willingly died for you centuries before you were conceived in your mother's womb. And I would die for you again, as often as might be necessary, if by dying I could win your love and your salvation.

Trust me, then, as a child trusts its mother, knowing that I cannot possibly wish you anything but good. Let your trust know no bounds and you will be at peace.

I have said, "He who does not accept the kingdom of God as a little child does will never enter it."[5] As a child accepts the "kingdom" of his parents—their rule, their authority, their love—so you must accept the kingdom of God.

What does a child do that I commend so highly?

He loves to be with his parents. When they are about to leave him, he says, "Take me with you!"; So also you should love to be with me, to speak to me, to think of me, wherever you may be, whatever you may be doing. I never willingly leave you; it is you who neglect me, ignore me, and drive me away from you by mortal sin.

A little child trusts his parents with unbounded confidence in their love and their power. When he wants a piece of bread, a glass of milk, he asks, confident of getting it. So, too, should you ask me with the utmost trust for your needs. Loving parents give children the best they have and I give you the best I have.

A little child, so long as his parents are close by, has no fears. When he awakes in the middle of the night he comes almost unthinkingly to their bed. So also you in all difficulties should turn spontaneously to me, fearing nothing in the sure knowledge that I am near.

The little child loves to climb on his parents' laps, to listen to their stories, to play all kinds of games with them; whatever his parents do delights him. Let this be your attitude toward your God; whatever I do, whatever I send to you, should delight you.

The little child knows that his parents' word is to be obeyed. In the same way my word, and that of my Church, is law and must be obeyed.

As the little child accepts his father and mother as king and queen of the home, so also you must accept your God as the King and Father of the whole universe and my immaculate Mother as its Queen.

Do you begin now to see why I have said, "He who does not accept the kingdom of God as a little child does will never enter it"?

The one possession that is yours is your will. What I want is the free, unrestricted, wholehearted, trusting gift of yourself. This is what a little child gives to his parents. An older child craving independence wants to exercise his own will. Natural as this is for the growing child, it is not the example upon which I desire your spiritual life to be modeled. The little child is your model, for he accepts the will of his parents in all things.

He does not fully understand, but neither does he question, because he trusts.

I too would be better satisfied with less "understanding" from my children, and far less "questioning."

Come to me, then, as a child to its father and mother. Are you sick, hungry, thirsty, troubled, grieved? Tell me, as you would your mother or father if you were a little child. You owe me this trust; it is my due.

Did I not trust my creatures enough to become man? Can you do less than trust me enough to give yourself over to me, your God, now and always, completely and without question?

My Father entrusted his only-begotten Son to mankind. Should not parents, then, entrust their sons and daughters to me and to my loving care?

Come to me, all you who are heavily laden, and I will refresh you. Trust in my overwhelming and merciful love. The greater your need, the deeper your grief and trouble, the more you should cling to me, and say "Lord, your will be done, your blessed will be done."

Christ Helps His Children

I myself will comfort you.

ISAIAH 51:12

A little child's greatest strength is its weakness. Because it is weak and helpless, its parents lavish their care and protection upon it. So, too, your greatest strength is your weakness. The more you distrust yourself and trust in me, the more surely will I help you to stand. The more you realize that you are nothing, the more you shall receive of me, who am everything. Your need is the measure of my support. Never allow your failings to discourage you, but use them to reach a more perfect union with me.

There are some who say, "I am not meant to be holy. I will never be a saint." How foolish! Is there a limit to what I can do, an end to my mercy? Do I not know your weaknesses? Shall I who made the eye not see your needs? Shall I who made the ear not hear your cry?

Your imperfections do not wound me; indeed, the more you struggle against them for my sake, the more they endear you to me. But the failure of your trust—this is the failing that hurts.

Strive to do my will, therefore, with joy and serenity. Avoid falls with all care, but never be discouraged. No matter how often or how far you fall, trust in my love.

When you come to me with childlike trust, I can refuse you nothing. A parent is quick to forgive and forget a child's forgetfulness, negligence, or thoughtless offense, and I forgive and forget your falls and failings even more quickly. Lift your mind to me, give me a glance, offer me something of yourself, and all is right. Confess your blackest sins in sorrow and your soul becomes white as snow.

Be as the child who, having failed and been forgiven, runs off blithely, completely forgetful of the past.

To do this is not only a secret of spiritual advancement, it is a sign of spiritual progress.

Do not be so wrapped up in yourself that you refuse to let the past die. Do not be angry with yourself for having given way to anger, disconsolate because your fall proves to you that you are not as good as you had thought. If at times I withdraw from you a little, permit you to test your own strength, and allow you to fall, it is to show you your weakness and how much you depend on me. Peter fell, denying me three times, because he trusted in himself and not in me.

Good parents are careful to watch over their children. They protect them against foreseen dangers, smoothing the path so that their little ones will not stumble and be hurt.

I, too, am near, alert, my hand outstretched to guard you against evils that threaten you. A thousand times a day I smooth your way and strengthen you with my grace. I turn on the light of understanding so that you may see your way, as a parent turns on the light to guide the child along a path at night.

I know you so well, I am familiar with all your ways. You cannot speak a word that I have not known from all eternity. I created your inner being, fashioned you in your mother's womb. Where can you flee from my spirit, from my presence? If you take up the wings of the dawn, if you dwell at the end of the sea, even there my hand will hold you fast. If you say, "Darkness shall cover me, and night shall surround me," darkness itself is not dark to me, and night shines as the day. To me darkness is as light.

I see you always and I love you always. Have confidence then, as a little child. As you hope and trust, so shall you receive. Never fear that you can ask too much of me. Such humility is not humility, but lack of trust. To you I say as to my Apostles, "Why are you so timid? How is it you are still without faith?"[6]

Sanctify Each Moment

> The Lord is . . . holy in all his works.
>
> PSALM 144:17

Abandonment to my divine will and the practice of spiritual childhood are immense sources of grace, of divine life.

You know that I have planned the circumstances of your entire life for you in every smallest detail. Every moment, then, every situation, every action of your life (sin alone excepted) is a means whereby you may enrich the divine life of your soul.

Every moment is, in a sense, a "sacrament," though not, of course, one of the seven sacraments, which are particular signs instituted by me to give grace. Nevertheless, all that happens to you, every moment of your life (sin excepted) may be regarded as a "sign" given to you, or permitted by me, to confer divine life upon you through your proper use of it. It is a means whereby you may unite yourself more closely with me.

Do you have a headache, a cold, a disappointment that afflicts you? Are you tempted, fatigued, sad? Is the weather too hot or too cold, too wet or too dry? Is your work too hard? Is it boring, producing no results? Are you anxious or afraid? These are all means of grace and in that sense they are "sacraments."

But it is not only the sorrows, pains, and disappointments of life that are sacraments of the moment. Your joys also are sources of grace. Your laughter at a joke, your pleasure at a movie or a game, your enjoyment of good food—all these are sources of divine life. Accept them, *will* them, as coming from my hands, as being part of my all-wise plan for your eternal happiness. It pleases me when you are delighted with my gifts.

As often as you can, therefore, call to mind such thoughts as these:

> This moment is given to me by my Lord that I may show my love for him by uniting my will with his. I could have nothing better than this specific opportunity to serve my Creator in this particular way. This trial, this interruption, this reprimand are permitted by my Lord to strengthen me and to unite me more closely to him. This movie, this game, this program are to relax my mind, to give me joy. All these are sacraments of the present moment, gifts of God's providence. If I use them well they will increase God's life in me.

I shall help you to call these thoughts to your mind. I shall help you to do whatever you should, thoroughly, happily, without worry, with no undue concern. I shall help you to say to me, "Lord, not only do I accept this moment with its exact and most minute circumstances, I *will* it because it is your will."

You know that I have said the truth shall make you free. This is the truth: *every moment is a sacrament* when your will is one with mine.

Union with my will makes you free; disharmony with my will makes you a slave.

Unite your will with mine and you will not fret about anything: the inadvertent remark that might have offended your neighbor, what others think of you, your financial condition, success or failure in your work, the security of your position, your health, the way the country is being governed, not even the extent of your progress in the spiritual life. You will not feel that you must run the universe; you will understand that I control it, in all matters, big and small. You will not desire to know what is ahead for you, but you will be content to leave the future in my hands. You will be concerned only with doing and cheerfully grasping my will and making it yours *at this moment*—because you trust the Maker of all, who is all-powerful, all-good, and all-love. You will be free because you possess the truth.

Do not waste these sacraments of the present moment. Order your life to my will as a good musician conforms and orders his playing to the will of the conductor. Submit to my tempo, my beat, my direction. Keep your eyes on me, as the musician keeps his eye on the leader. How else can you know my will? Turn to me often in thought, prayer, and recollection.

Say to me:

> At this and every moment. I trust you, dear Lord, for you are all-powerful.
> At this and every moment, I trust you, for you are goodness itself.
> At this and every moment, I trust you, for you live in me, and I in you.

At this and every moment, I trust you, for you
    are my brother and for me you gave your life.
At this and every moment, I trust you, for your
    Father is my Father.
At this and every moment, I trust you, for your
    Mother is my Mother.
At this and every moment, I trust you. You have
    given yourself to me, can I do less for you?
At this and every moment, I trust you. You love
    me, do I not also love you?
At this and every moment, I trust you. You wish
    to give me even more than I wish to receive.
At this and every moment, I trust you. I will
    never grieve you by hesitation, because
    hesitation implies that I doubt you.
At this and every moment, I trust you, not
    because I am good but because you are perfect.
At this and every moment, I trust you, not
    because I am strong but because you are
    omnipotent.

O my God! I will this moment in all its circumstances. It is your will; therefore it is my will. I
want at this moment nothing more than I have—
and nothing less. In your infinite wisdom, you
have seen fit to bring me to this moment of my
existence, possessing certain strengths and many
weaknesses. I thank you for my strengths. I
praise you for my weaknesses. You have given
me abilities in the measure that is best for me.
You have allowed me to have weaknesses in the

measure that accords with Your eternal plan for me. I will it all, because it is all your will.

I do not wish at this moment to be stronger than I am. My weaknesses serve your glory. If through them I shall fall in the future, let me learn humility. If I shall be miserable, let me offer you my misery—and let it give glory to your justice. If my misdeeds bring punishment upon me, this, too, will be to your glory, for it is just that wickedness should be punished.

But O my God, protect me, I beg you. O my strength, to you will I sing praise, for you are my defense, O God, my mercy.

chapter three

BE WHAT I DESIRE

Accept Your Position in Life

> One has to be content with what has been
> assigned him by heaven.
>
> JOHN 3:27

If you observe faithfully the first of my rules for holiness and happiness—complete *abandonment to my will*—I will surely lead you also to persevere in the second rule, which is: *Be what I desire.*

So many feel that they would be happy if only they had money, popularity, talents, or fame. Do you? Are you quite certain that these "gifts" would be good for you? Are you sure that you know what is good for you? Do you know your needs as well as I know them?

To be what I desire you must first learn to accept your present state in life, your personality and all your circumstances, joyfully, gaily, with carefree abandon. It is not difficult to see my will in the Ten Commandments, the precepts of my Church, and even in the commands of those who are over you in civil and economic affairs. But it is sometimes very hard for you to see my will in what I permit to happen to you. Yet you know that I desire only your happiness. I have planned your happiness. The gifts that I give are best for you.

Never fear that I do not know what I am doing. The path to sainthood, and happiness, is not the same for all. Do not be downcast at the comparison between what you do and what Teresa, Francis of Assisi, Dominic, Camillus, Peter Claver, Catherine of Siena, the Curé of Ars, and John Bosco did.

I do not tell you to emulate them in their individual practices, at any rate, not now. Later, perhaps, I may ask more of you; but all in my good time. What I do ask, now and always, is that you imitate them in their love for me, that you trust me by accepting joyously the state of life in which you find yourself, and that you conform yourself to it. Abandon your will to mine as they did—be what I desire as they were—and you, too, will become as truly holy as they are.

Parents sometimes become so engrossed in social work or in church work, not to mention their professions, that they flee from the family circle night after night, forsaking the primary duty that I have given them for a secondary interest that they have given themselves.

How blind they are! They would serve me as the saints did, but they forget that the saints became saints by serving me in the work I gave them.

I do not wish you to be famous, rich, talented, or popular at this time—unless you are. I do not wish you to be married at this time—unless you are. I do not wish you to be a martyr or to nurse the sick in hospitals, to give all your wealth to the poor, to spend nights in contemplative prayer—unless these things conform to your state in life. Should I be pleased to have you care for the sick in hospitals and neglect the sick or the young that I have given you to care for in your own home? Should I be happy to have you serve the aged outside, but neglect the aged that I have placed within your own family circle?

John Bosco had to go to the streets and alleys to find children to train in my ways. But in so many homes today parents forego their opportunity to guide their own flesh and blood into union with me.

I desire husbands and wives first and foremost to love one another and be the best husbands and wives they can. I desire mothers and fathers to guide their children with love and patience and be the best mothers and fathers they can. If the poor are not succored, and the sick not nursed, and if the faithful do not have the Gospel preached to them, these are not your failures and responsibilities, except as these works conform to your state in life. But if husbands, wives, and children see in you an example that is less than Christlike, that is your failure.

On the other hand, many who have time, opportunity, and ability to serve me in their neighbor neglect doing so. They confine themselves to a personal spirituality that excludes their neighbor. Such selfish spirituality is not what I desire.

I have given you tasks and talents that are fitted to you. Just as birds are made to fly and fish to live in water, so man is made to seek God, and each one in a particular way. One is a parent, another a priest; one a ditchdigger, another a doctor; one serves me best in learning, another in ignorance.

Learn of my Apostle Paul, who admonished: "If a man is a prophet, let him prophesy as far as the measure of his faith will let him. The administrator must be content with his administration, the teacher with his work of teaching, the preacher with his preaching. Each must perform his own task well. . . ."[1]

Do not spend your time in dreaming what you would do if you were someone else or in another state of life. Accept your present situation in all its circumstances.

Acceptance, however, does not mean passivity. If you are sick, accept it as my will for the moment; but ordinarily it is not my will that you should do nothing to get well. Do not complain, but take reasonable measures to cure your illness. In the same way, if your present situation is unsatisfactory, accept it willingly, without complaint, for now; but strive to improve it in reasonable, common-sense ways. This is being what I desire. It is doing my will as I would have it done.

Seek the Virtues of Your Calling

> Learn where is wisdom, where is strength,
> where is understanding. . . .
>
> BARUCH 3:14

You have but one real present duty: to serve me as I desire to be served, in the situation wherein I have allowed you to be placed. Within this one supreme duty, you have, of course, secondary responsibilities: to yourself, to your family, to your employer or superior, and to society itself. Try to fulfill all these responsibilities; but do not give too much of yourself to what is less important at the cost of giving too little to what is more important.

For a family man or woman, the family comes before the job or the career: yes, even before private prayers and devotions. For a child, obedience comes first. This is my plan. This is my example. When I was twelve years of age, just coming into manhood according to the custom of the time, I went to the Temple and took my place in the midst of those who taught there. I might have begun my public work at that time, but seeing my Mother's wish, I returned to Nazareth and for eighteen years I stayed there and was "subject" as fitted my state in life.

What I am teaching you is that you should seek the virtues that conform to your present situation, rather than those which may be more attractive to your fancy.

There are particular virtues for particular callings. The parent has great need of patience in dealing with his children. The husband and wife have special need of love in living so closely together. The child has particular need of obedience. A priest needs virtues of one sort, a nun of another, a businessman of another, a doctor of still another. There are special applications of the same virtue for each state in life. It is a counsel of perfection, as well as charity to an extraordinary degree, to give all one's wealth to the poor. But the same virtue of charity forbids the father with family dependents to sell all he has and give it to the poor; rather, charity requires that he take reasonable and ordinary measures to provide adequately for his family.

I command you to pray. But I would far rather see a wife and mother in the kitchen cooking and scrubbing, when it is time for cooking and scrubbing, than kneeling before me in the Blessed Sacrament.

Do you think that I look on you with disfavor for performing the duties I have given you? I am far closer to you when you are busy with the duties of your state in life because you know this is my will, even though you have no direct thought of me in your mind, than I could ever be while you were giving me all your attention in prayer but knowingly neglecting the duties of your state in life.

Your work, done out of love and obedience for me, is truly prayer. It is prayer in the concrete, love in action.

Do you understand now what I mean when I say that you must practice the virtues that conform to your duty, rather than those that appeal to your fancy if you are to be what I desire?

The religious has his or her rule of life. The husband, the wife, the mother, the father, the unmarried, the child each has his rule of life also: the duties of his state.

Accept your present situation and carry out its responsibilities, even as I accepted my situation and my responsibilities centuries ago in Palestine.

Are you weighed down by monotony? I was. Accept it!

Are you misunderstood? I was. Accept it!

Are you sometimes discouraged by the failure of your plans? Was it not discouraging for me on the day before my death to find my own Apostles quarreling over who among them should have the first place? Was it not discouraging for me to be rejected by those I came to save? Accept it!

Are you often disappointed by those with whom you must work and live? Was it not disappointing for me to hand-pick twelve special followers, only to see one of them become first a thief, then a traitor? Accept it!

Does your present state sometimes plunge you into circumstances wherein your sorrow seems almost greater than you can bear? Compare it with my sorrow that night in Gethsemani when the burden of all the sins of mankind descended upon my heart so that in my agony my blood broke through the pores of my skin and dripped down my face and neck to the ground. Accept it!

Accept your present situation. It is best for you at this time. The children I have given to parents—and the parents I have given to children—are best for each other. These particular children and these particular parents are part of my plan. This particular employer or superior, and this particular employee or inferior, are best for each other at this time. Tomorrow, it may be different. Today, they have each a purpose to serve in this special situation.

Be what I desire.

Accept your position in my plan. And I say to you that your path shall become a path of kindness and faithfulness. For my eyes rest on those who seek my way that I may lead them to joy.

In Your Daily Work

> Serve the Lord in truth, and seek to do the
> things that please him.
>
> Tobit 14:10

I desire that your days should be filled with the joy and peace that I have left to you as your inheritance.

Your one concern is to do my will moment by moment in the tasks and circumstances that fall to you. Do that, and all else follows my divine plan for your happiness today and every day into eternity.

Do not allow yourself to become too concerned with the success of what you do in your daily tasks. Do not be afraid to fail. Many times you put off doing something that is your duty because you fear that you will not be able to do it properly.

Ask yourself, "What does my Lord desire?" Then do exactly that. Do not postpone it from day to day. I do not say that you need not prepare; but you yourself know only too well the difference between preparing and putting off. One of my saints, Augustine, said: "God has promised us forgiveness for our mistakes; he has not promised us tomorrow for our procrastination."

Desire to do no other work than that which is your duty at any particular moment. Say to me, "Lord, I will this task because this task is your will for me at this time."

Attack the tasks you dread doing—out of love for me. I will give you the grace to remember that you need not hurry or wear yourself out or rush about on a time schedule. I will help you to smile and be serene. Work calmly and peacefully, doing as much as you can accomplish in that manner, and stop when you become fatigued and ineffective.

Ordinarily, I do not want you to work so long or so hard that you become cross.

Work with care and diligence, but not with worry or anxiety. You can be careful and diligent and, at the same time, tranquil and serene. But you cannot be at peace or work well when you attack your tasks with uneasiness and anxious fretfulness.

Do you recall that I admonished Martha at her home in Bethany because she was troubled about many things? I did not admonish her because she was busy, or because she was diligent, but because she was troubled. Do not let yourself be troubled.

I would have you do your daily tasks without feverish haste, indeed, with leisure. Do them calmly and peaceably, one at a time, not seeking to do all of them at once. I have made the day twenty-four hours, with a time

for work and a time for rest. The day is just long enough
for you to do what I want you to do, provided you lead a
reasonably ordered life and seek only my will.

Heed these words of one of my saints:

> Imitate little children, who, as they with one hand
> hold fast to their father, with the other gather
> strawberries or blackberries along the hedges. So
> too, as you gather and handle the goods of this
> world with one hand, you must with the other
> always hold fast the hand of your heavenly Father
> turning yourself towards him from time to time to
> see if your actions or occupations be pleasing to
> him. . . . Amidst those ordinary affairs and occupa-
> tions which do not require so sharp and earnest an
> attention, you should look more on God than on
> them. When they are of such importance as to
> require your whole attention for doing them well,
> then also you should look from time to time
> toward God. . . . Thus will God work with you, in
> you, and for you, and your labor shall be followed
> with consolations.[2]

Even though you work diligently, you will not
always succeed. Your best efforts will not always meet
with the approval of your fellow men. Do not let this
upset you. Offer your natural disappointment to me.
Tell me that since this disappointment is occurring
with my permission you would not change it if you
could; tell me that you desire it, that you will it. There
is something about offering your disappointment to
me that is like putting a soothing lotion on a sore or
cut; it stings, but soon the injury feels better.

Do the task of the moment thoroughly, for the love of my Father, the Holy Spirit, and me. Do not perform it half-heartedly, thinking meanwhile that you will do the task of tomorrow, or of the next hour, perfectly. Do this present action perfectly, out of as a pure a love for the Trinity as you are capable. To drive a car, take a walk, prepare a meal, study a lesson, endure a rebuke, enjoy a game, and to do so thoroughly and well because that is what I wish you to do at that moment is the highest praise you can possibly offer.

Yes, to go to sleep at night, though willing or even preferring to stay up, because that is what I wish you to do at that time, and to do it solely for love, is better than spending the night in prayer if to do so would make you too tired the next day to do your work properly.

This, then, is how you shall be what I desire you to be in all your daily occupations. In the morning, make an act of abandonment, of complete trust, that whatever happens that day happens only by my permission. Recall that every moment is a "sacrament," every incident a means of grace. Renew this act of abandonment frequently during the day; a mere word, a glance in my direction, is enough.

Resolve not to hurry in your tasks. Resolve to do all things calmly, perseveringly, not worrying or hastening to finish, and above all not being too concerned about what others may think. *Do one thing at a time.* And do all things as much as possible solely for me.

Do this and you will be what I desire!

Purity of Intention

> Do everything for God's glory.
>
> 1 CORINTHIANS 10:31

Accomplishments of themselves are very slight in my eyes. Actions without love are nothing. Love is everything. My saints have realized this and have said that to pick up a pin for the pure love of God is a greater deed than to preach brilliant sermons out of mixed love. The worth of an act, like the worth of a gift, in my estimation is measured by the love which prompts it. Therefore, the little child can give me gifts as great as those of kings—and greater if its love is purer than that of kings. That is why anyone who loves me can serve me even to the pinnacle of sanctity.

Try not to dilute the worth of your gifts of action by mixing the love of God with the love of human respect, or the love of praise, honors, or profits. Not that it is wrong to act from such natural motives, but they are insufficient, and your goal is pure love. Do what you do, so far as you can, solely for the love of God, without any other considerations whatsoever.

Keep your intentions pure; above all desire to serve me in the way I give you at this moment. Never forget that it is for me that you work; not for success, not for human plaudits, not for earthly rewards. I say again, do not become too engrossed in the work itself. If you work for me it does not really matter whether or not success rewards your efforts. Leave all this in my hands. Since I do not need your labor, the result is of little consequence; all that matters is that you did it for me. This is very important and that is why I repeat it so often. Try very hard to understand this point. Think on it!

Some who desire ardently to do my will worry about what *is* my will. I do not want you to worry about this or anything else. I do not want you to spend anxious moments in deciding, for example, whether to pray the Rosary or to read the Scripture, whether to read a book or take a walk, whether to call on the sick or visit me. Some of my friends spend more time in deciding than in the action itself. Heed the words of Francis de Sales: "We are to proportion our attention to the importance of what we undertake. . . . We must walk in good faith and . . . freely choose as we like, so as not to weary our spirit, lose our time, or put ourselves in danger of disquiet, scruples, and superstition."[3]

Though I am always guiding you, I give you great freedom. If you cannot make up your mind between two courses of action, neither of them of major importance, do not continue too long in debate. Choose one or the other and abide by your decision.

Even in important things do not delay so long that you lose your peace of mind. You cannot force me to reveal my will. Sometimes I do not want you to see your way too clearly; then, you must choose in the dark as best as you can. Simply pray to the Holy Spirit to enlighten you, calmly consider the matter, consult those whose opinions you respect, and make your decision. Choose, and do not afterward quibble and debate your choice.

Having made it, peacefully and steadfastly pursue it, acting always with the pure intention of doing my will.

Do not doubt that you are doing my will, once you have holily and reasonably formed your resolution.

This does not mean that you are infallibly right in your choice so far as human wisdom is concerned. A parent may make a wrong decision as regards the welfare of the family, and yet make it with my blessing. But you are always infallibly right spiritually, that is, so far as your soul's profit is concerned, when you have earnestly and humbly sought my divine will in your decision.

No matter what happens as the result, no matter if things or men make you suffer, you have done well. Think not of your sufferings, but think of me, for by these events or these men I am striving to make you more surely one with me. Say to me, "Behold the servant of the Lord; be it done to me according to your will."

Unite your will with mine in little things, constantly, all day long, saying over and over, "Thy kingdom come, Thy will be done." Do this faithfully in small matters and you will find it easy to unite your will with mine in big things, for whosoever is loyal in little matters will be so also in larger ones.

Thus you will give me your all, which is what I desire: your life, your prayers, your work, your play, your reading, your study, your walking, your thinking, your eating, and even your sleeping. At the base of all will be the simple, pure intention of living according to my plan for you.

Painting Christ's Portrait

> Put on the Lord Jesus Christ. . . .
>
> ROMANS 13:14

Your work, my dear friend, is to paint a portrait. Your happiness now and forever depends on it. Whose portrait? mine.

How?

With your life.

My Father has given you canvas, brushes, paints, a room to work in, a Subject to reproduce. The canvas is your life; the brushes are your thoughts, words, and deeds; the paints are the inspirations, temptations, trials, and joys you encounter; the room is your vocation in life; and I am the Subject.

Fashion your life so that when my Father looks on you he will see my image.

Let me help you. I am eager for you to "put on Christ," so that I may live in you and you in me, so that you may partake more fully of my nature who did partake of your nature.

To help you do this, I became a true man, a whole man, from birth to death. I have shown you how God wants man to live.

Strive to imitate especially those virtues of mine that are most necessary for your state in life. This is how you will "put on Christ." This is how you will allow me to live in you more fully.

Learn all you can about me. Familiarize yourself with my life. Try to "see" me as I walked the roads and

fields of Palestine nineteen centuries ago. I am truly
man and truly God; therefore I can truly be your
model.

My disciples loved me, and I loved them. They felt
comfortable, "at home" with me. We talked frankly;
Peter sometimes argued with me, and Judas grumbled
in my presence. My disciples brought their quarrels to
me to be settled.

Sometimes I tested them to see how they would
act, just as I test you. Once, crossing the Sea of Galilee,
I slept in the rear of the boat while a storm raged about
us. They made their way back to me, shook me, and
cried out somewhat reproachfully, "Rabbi! We are
going down! Is that nothing to you?"[4] I calmed the
winds and the waves. And afterward I said to them,
"Why are you so timid? Where is your faith?"[5] How
often, when you have doubted or mistrusted me, have
I had occasion to ask you, "Where is your faith? Why
were you afraid?"

Another time, when thousands of people had followed us into the wilderness and stayed until it grew
late, my disciples said, "This is a lonely place, and it is
already late . . . dismiss the people so that they can
reach the farms and villages round about and buy themselves something to eat."[6] "They have no need to go
away," I said, "it is for you to give them something to
eat."[7] Philip answered, with his characteristic frankness,
"Bread for two hundred denarii [about 35 dollars' worth]
is not enough for each of them to get even a little."[8]

I told my disciples to see what food was available
and Andrew reported, "There is a lad here who has five

barley loaves and two fish; but what is that for so many?"⁹ I had them bring me the loaves and the fish, and I had the people sit down. They distributed the food, all were fed, and the fragments left over filled twelve baskets.

I was testing their faith. All the time I knew precisely what I would do. Many times have I tested your faith just so, always knowing precisely what I would do.

Study my life. It will reveal to you that I am indeed a complete man, a whole man, a real man. It will prove to you that my disciples were normal men, leading normal lives.

Meditate upon it. Try to see it.

See the poor man who has lain thirty-eight years beside the pool of Bethsaida and whom I heal. I have compassion for him, even as you do for the cripples you encounter. He does not even have to ask me to cure him. I ask him whether he wants to be made well. And when he replies that he has no one to place him in the pool, I cure him.

See the widow outside the gates of Naim and her dead son, whom I give back to her. Neither does she have to ask. My heart melts at her sorrow just as yours would have done.

See the woman who has been eighteen years bent over and unable to look up, whom I straighten and cure.

See the woman who has hemorrhaged for twelve years, who touches my garment and is healed.

See Mary, Martha, and the others standing before the tomb of Lazarus, my friend, whom I call back from death.

See the man who has been blind from birth, to whom I give sight.

See the twelve-year-old daughter of Jairus, whom I raise from death.

See the centurion pleading for his son, whom I cure; the man with the withered hand, whom I heal; Peter's mother-in-law, whose fever I check; the servant of the high priest, whose ear Peter cut off in Gethsemani and whom I make whole.

See my mercy toward the souls of the afflicted: the adulteress, the paralytic, and Mary Magdalene.

See my indignation at hypocrisy and injustice.

See how I take note of the needs of the body: feeding the multitudes and providing the wine at Cana.

See how I mingle with all classes: banqueting with rich Pharisees, supping with public sinners.

See how I plead for my executioners as they nail me to the cross: "Father, forgive them; they do not know what they are doing."[10]

See how I promise the poor thief who is crucified with me, "This very day you will be with me in paradise."[11]

See all this and strive to imitate my virtues: such normal, everyday virtues as patience, mildness, kindness, mercy, forgiveness, love.

Following Christ

> We . . . have given up everything and have
> become your followers.
>
> Mark 10:28

Let me explain to you exactly what you must do to be what I desire.

You must faithfully perform all your daily duties, big and little, out of love for me. Remember that these are the duties I have given you. They are "sacraments" of the moment. Thus you will have the right disposition for me to live in you.

You must pray for the grace to imitate me more closely, to understand me more fully, to unite your will with mine more firmly. Ask for this grace, here and now. Ask for it every day.

You must be faithful in assisting at Mass and receiving the sacraments; do so as often as your position and circumstances in life permit. Especially when I come to you in my sacrament of the Eucharist, appeal to me to make you into my likeness. I cannot refuse you. I will it even more than you do. Ask, and you shall receive in greatest abundance the graces you need. I long to cause the love with which I love the Father to spring from my soul into yours, to live in you and grow in you and ripen into heavenly fruit.

You must study me. Read the Gospels especially, reflecting on my attributes every day and on the majesty and power and love that are God's. Compare, as best you can, your faint replica of goodness with the infinite goodness of the Almighty. Look at your actions. Why do you do them? Because they are my Father's will, or because they serve your self-love? Even your best actions, how far short they fall of my goodness! Compare what you do and how you do it with what I did and how I did it.

Reflect on my goodness and love as man and as God. If, as man, I taught, healed, and even died for my brothers, what must be my goodness and love as God? If, as man, I gave to the utmost, does it not follow that as God I also give to the utmost? And who can limit God?

Is there anything that I could do as man that I have not done for you? Is there, then, anything that I will not do as God? Meditate, and you will see what I have given for you on earth, even to my death on the cross; yet you cannot even faintly imagine what I do for you in the court of heaven.

As you strive to emulate me, you will have both successes and failures. Do not be proud of your successes, but equally important do not be downcast by your failures. You are human, therefore you are weak. Because I was human, I fell beneath my cross on the way to Calvary. I accepted my human weakness because it was my Father's will. I did not have to accept it; I did not need to fall; but having become man I was obedient to the limitations of my humanity.

Understand that no amount of suffering, not even death itself, could have redeemed you. Love redeemed you, the love I have for my Father.

I wish you to accept your humanity with its weaknesses and limitations. No matter how many or how great your imperfections, they do not matter, provided they are involuntary. I wish you even to glory in your imperfections, knowing that you please me greatly by accepting them with humility. Unite your falls with mine beneath the weight of the cross. Offer them to me with all their humiliations. Offer to me your weakness; I shall deem it a fitting gift.

How shall you imitate me and be what I desire? Pray, study, and imitate the virtues you find in me. Be humble, pure, patient, kind. Be full of love for God and your neighbor. Above all, unite your will with mine as I united mine with that of my Father. I have no other will but his. You should have no other will but mine. This is the essence of love.

Do your daily tasks, then, with love. I do not look so much to what you do as to the love with which you do it. Out of love for me, out of a selfless will to do my will, be kind to your neighbors, obedient to your superiors, generous to those who are below or weaker than you. Be patient, calm, and cheerful. Do what you should with a smiling countenance and a light heart.

In all things practice my virtues, but especially the union of our wills. This is being what I desire. This is partaking of my nature. This is painting my portrait.

chapter four

CHRIST IN US

The Mystical Body of Christ

> I am the vine, you are the branches.
>
> JOHN 15:5

Now, my dear friend, I will tell you plainly some awesome truths.

I, with my whole Church, am one mystical person. My Church and I form one Mystical Body which is, in the words of Augustine, the whole Christ.

You cannot comprehend this mystery, nor can human words express it. You can only approach its meaning dimly through analogies.

Your body has many parts, yet it is one. You have a head, a mouth, a nose, eyes and ears, arms and legs, hands and feet. All these parts have different functions, yet they all form one body animated by one soul. Let your eye suffer and the whole body is distressed. Let the pangs of hunger be assuaged and the whole body shares the pleasure.

Somewhat as your body has many, parts and yet is one whole, so my Mystical Body consists of many members, each with a separate function, and yet is one. I am the Head of this Body, the Holy Spirit is its Soul, and the faithful of my Church are its living members.

As the branch of a tree contains the life of the tree within itself, so you contain my life. As many grains of wheat unite to make one loaf of bread, and many drops of water combine to make a sea, so also many individuals in my Church are incorporated into one Mystical Body, which is myself. That is why Paul could write, "True, I am living, here and now, this mortal life; but my real life is the faith I have in the Son of God. . . ."[1] And again, "All you who have been baptized in Christ's name have put on the person of Christ . . . you are all one person in Jesus Christ."[2] And that is why I said to him as he hunted down the members of my Church, "Saul, Saul, why do you persecute me?"[3]

As a member of my Mystical Body you are one with me. You live in me and I live in you. You dwell in the Father and he in you. You dwell in the Holy Spirit and he also in you. You dwell in the Trinity and the Trinity dwells in you.

I am I, and you are you—separate and distinct persons—yet we are one. Such is your dignity, O Christian.

How can this be? What does it mean?

It does not mean that you are God. Neither you nor any member of my Church passes beyond the sphere of creatures because of this union. It does not mean that you are joined to my human body so that a new physical person is created. My Mystical Body is not a physical body. It does not mean that you lose your own personality, your free will, your responsibility for your thoughts, words, and deeds.

Nevertheless, my Mystical Body, though not physical, is real. It is not imaginary or allegorical.

There are higher forms of oneness than physical oneness. The principle of union that binds together the members of my Church and me is immeasurably superior to the bonds of union which bind together the parts of any physical body. There are no words to describe adequately our oneness in this relationship. As a member of my Mystical Body you are more closely united to me than you were to your own mother when you were in her womb. And I am more closely united to you than I was to my own Mother in the natural order when I was in her womb.

You must understand that this oneness is in the supernatural order. You possess a twofold life, the natural and the supernatural, the life of a rational animal and the divine life of God.

Because my Mystical Body is in the supernatural order, neither time nor space confine it. And this fact makes possible the wondrous truth that has changed

your entire destiny. Since my Mystical Body is not confined by time I could die for your sins before you had
committed them. I could, in a sense, live your life for
you before you were conceived. Since my Mystical
Body is not confined by space, I can include in it all
Christians simultaneously.

As man, I enjoyed the beatific vision from the time
I was received in my Mother's womb. In that vision I
have forever and continuously had present to myself
all the members of my Mystical Body. Never did I
cease to embrace them in my love. In the temple of my
Mother's body, in the workshop of Nazareth, in the
byways of Palestine, on the cross, in the eternal glory
of my Father, I saw and embraced you and all the
members of my Church, and this I did with a clarity
and a charity immeasurably superior to the knowledge
and love of a mother for her child—even the love and
knowledge of my Mother for me.

Can you now begin dimly to understand the awesome truth of my Mystical Body? Because I held you in
my gaze and my love at all times, every moment of my
life is connected with every moment of yours. All of
my life is in a sense at your disposal every moment of
your life. At any instant I am ready to make right all
that is wrong. You have only to unite your will with
mine and this unites your life with mine. Each tick of
the clock gives you a new opportunity to lose your
poverty in my superabundance.

This is what it means to be of my Mystical Body.
Though our union is not in the physical order, through
this mystical union we are more surely one than your

hand or foot, your arm or leg is one with your own body. We are one true Organism, one true Mystical Body, and that Body is myself.

The Dignity of a Christian

> I in them and you in me.
>
> JOHN 17:23

At the moment when I offered myself to the Father, in my passion and death, mankind's mystical union with me came into being. At that moment my Mystical Body was born; At that moment, even though you were not to be born for many centuries, your own mystical union with me came into existence potentially.

Your union with me became actual the moment you received faith and baptism. As the cleansing water trickled upon your head and the purifying words were spoken, my life permeated your soul. Possessing my life, you lived in me and I in you. My Father instantaneously accepted you as his adopted child, making you coheir with me to the kingdom of heaven. From that moment, you became one with me; *my crucifixion became your crucifixion; my death on the cross, your death; my right to heaven, your right to heaven.*

At the instant of baptism and of faith in me, you became a sharer in my atonement, just as if you had died in atonement yourself. This is so because the grace that was given to me was given me not only as an individual but as the Head of the Church, so that this grace flows from me into my members. My actions have the same relation to myself and to my members as the actions of a man in the state of grace have to the man himself. Whatever I did is yours, as though you had done it yourself.

Because you have this oneness with me, I was able to atone by my death for original sin and for all your personal sins. I continue to make recompense for your sins by the renewal in the Mass of my death on the cross. You, too, are able to atone for your sins and those of others by offering yourself with me not only in the Mass, but in all your thoughts and deeds. You are able to be with me a coredeemer of the human race. Offering yourself, you are in a sense all mankind making sacrifice, all mankind making atonement.

Let me express this vital truth again. When I offered myself on the cross, I was not only Jesus, the Son of God and Son of Mary, making recompense; I was mankind making recompense; I was you making recompense. Again, in the Mass I am you making atonement, giving glory, praise, and thanksgiving to the Father. I sanctify you in myself. I am able to sanctify you in myself because you are mystically united to me. You are of my Mystical Body.

Realize your dignity. I partook of your human nature and you partake of my divine nature. You are human, yet God dwells in you. You are mortal, yet you have eternal life. You are you, and I am I, yet we are mystically one.

Realize also your responsibility. Your nature has been transformed, raised to a higher plane. Your life can no longer be merely natural; you live now on a supernatural level, a member of my Mystical Body. Doing my will, which is doing the Father's will, is the fundamental principle of union with my Mystical Body. Every act of conformity to my will is an act of union with me, an act of *communion*. Every act of rebellion against my will is a denial of union with me, an act of disunion. If the act of *dis*-union is grave and knowing and fully willful, then by it you destroy your supernatural life. You do not separate yourself from the Mystical Body, so long as you retain faith in me, but you are dead; you are a lifeless member of my Body, like a decayed limb of a tree or a cancerous cell of a human body.

Never let this happen. It is a tragedy beyond description.

Do you understand now why the unity of the divine life is far closer than the unity of human life? Do you see how it is that you are more closely united to me supernaturally than my own Mother is humanly united to me? Do you appreciate that all men who possess divine life, no matter what their color or nationality, are more closely related to one another than they are related by human nature even to their own parents?

Do you savor my meaning when in our first conversation I said: "He who does the will of my Father in heaven is my brother, my sister, my mother"?

All this is implicit in the prayer I addressed for you to my Father on the day before I died: "However, I do not pray for them [my Apostles] alone; I also pray for those who through their preaching will believe in me. All are to be one; just as you, Father, are in me and I am in you, so they, too, are to be one in us. . . . The glory you have bestowed on me I have bestowed on them, that they may be one as we are one—I in them and you in me. Thus their oneness will be perfected. The world must come to acknowledge that I am your ambassador, and that you love them as you love me. . . . May the love with which you love me dwell in them as I dwell in them myself."[4]

I will that all men may be one. The Father, the Son, and the Holy Spirit are three and yet we are one. All things are common between us. That you may be one in us, even as we are one: this is the dignity to which I have elevated you.

Christian, realize your dignity!

Christ Commands Us to Love

> Let your conduct be guided by love, as Christ
> also loved us. . . .
>
> EPHESIANS 5:2

Does the knowledge that you are so closely related to your fellow men in my Mystical Body inspire you with new love for your neighbor?

It should. It should give you new vision, new understanding, new love. I have left you a new commandment of love: to love your neighbor not merely as you love yourself, but even as I have loved you; to see in your neighbor not yourself, but me. The way you will show your love for me will be the love you bear your fellow man.

As I said to my first disciples, so I say to you: "If you love me, you will treasure my commandments. . . . This is my commandment: love one another as I love you. . . . That is all I command you: love one another."[5]

You find it hard to bear with the frailties of others, even your own family. On the night before my suffering and death, my dearest friends quarreled and bickered, each one anxious to be set above the others. But did I scold them, flay them with bitter words, scorch them with the fire of my indignation? No, I rose from my place, laid aside my outer garments, took a towel, poured water into a basin, and washed their feet.

When I had finished, I sat down again and I asked them, "Do you appreciate what I have just done to you? You call me 'Rabbi,' and 'Master'; and you are right. That is what I am. Well, then if I have washed your feet—I, the Master and Rabbi—you too ought to wash one another's feet."[6]

Follow my example!

You find it hard to put the welfare of others, even that of your dear friends, above your own. Your first thoughts are of and for yourself. One night the horror of sin and the natural aversion to pain and death weighed so heavily upon me that blood oozed through the pores of my skin. And my best friends slept, though I had asked them to watch with me. Yet I said to the guards, who came with weapons, torches, and lanterns to seize me, ". . . since you are looking for me, let these men go unmolested."[7]

Follow my example.

Do you give your time generously to others? Or do you shut your door against the unfortunate and close your ears to their pleas? Many a day, and many a night, the townspeople brought to me all who were distressed, so that the whole city gathered about. And I healed those that were afflicted with diseases of every sort.

Follow my example.

Do you love those who abuse you or do you strike back in anger? Picture a scene in Nazareth, where I have been preaching in the synagogue. My fellow townsmen scoff at me. They refuse to believe. They taunt me, telling me to work some miracles. I reason with them, reminding them of the proverb that a prophet has no honor in his own city and that they are making this proverb come true. I rebuke them for their stubborn pride. Enraged, they seize me and rush me to the brow of a hill and they are about to throw me over the cliff.

I can strike them down, slay them with a bolt of lightning, cause the earth to open and swallow them.

But they are my Father's creatures and I love them. I have come to save, not to destroy. I walk through the midst of them, so that this sin shall not be laid at their door.

I have given you an example.

Are you merciful? Can you be gentle and patient when you have a throbbing headache? Come to Calvary. Hear the clang of the hammers as they drive huge spikes through my wrists and feet. See the blood and the twitching of my tortured limbs.

"Father—Forgive them—they do not know what they are doing."[8]

Hear the jeering of the onlookers, the scoffing of the passers-by, the blasphemies of the robber on my left.

Now listen: the act of faith and contrition of the good thief, "Jesus, remember me. . . ."

And hear my glad answer, "I assure you, this very day you will be with me in Paradise."[9]

I have given you an example.

Consider the parables. There are a hundred sheep and one is lost. And the shepherd goes seeking that one sheep until, finding it, he carries it back on his shoulders, full of joy.

A woman has ten pieces of money, and she loses one. She hunts all over the house, and when she finds the lost piece she calls in her neighbors and all rejoice together.

A man has two sons. While one stays at home, the other takes his part of the inheritance and squanders it in riotous living in a far-off country. But when later he returns penniless to his father's house, his father receives him joyfully, clothes him in the best garments, puts his own ring on his finger, and has the best calf killed.

How many crimes that cry to heaven for vengeance are done every day! How many sheep are lost! Yet my Father seeks the sheep and spares the sinners, waiting for them as for a prodigal son. Do you also forgive those who offend you? Do you receive with joy the prodigals who seek you out to renew an injured friendship?

Love your fellow men as I have loved you. Show your love for me by your love for them. I say to you: Love, and forgive, and seek out others that you may serve them and me in them.

Christ In Others

> We . . . are one body in Christ.
>
> ROMANS 12:5

What is your attitude toward those who are discourteous, who infringe on your rights, who push you aside, who take advantage of you, who cheat and ridicule you? Do you follow the example I have given you?

Love your enemies. Do good to those that hate you, pray for those who persecute you and insult you. As my Father in heaven makes his sun shine on the evil and equally on the good, his rain fall on the just and equally on the unjust, so you must smile on all with true love, not only on your friends who do good to you, but on those who insult and hate and injure you. Seek them out. Show them kindness.

Do not be overcritical, looking for the defects of others rather than for their perfections. Resolve to go through this day without criticizing anyone except as duty requires.

When you are tempted to impatience and anger, think of this: to be irritable with others is, in a sense, to be irritable with me. I am in all members of my Mystical Body. And I love them, each and every one. If only one person had been barred from divine union by Adam's sin, I would have come to earth to redeem him. If I love all men so much, then you also must love them, every one. As I was ready to live and die for each of them, so you, if you would follow me perfectly, should be ready to live, or die if need be, for others. What you do for another, you do to and for me.

Sometimes it is your duty to admonish others. The child who does wrong must be reproved, but always in the spirit of love. Correct your child or anyone under your authority as my Mother corrected me. Regard him who needs counseling as a weary Christ to be helped, as the thirsty Christ at the well in Samaria or the suffering Christ hanging on the cross. As Veronica with kindness and love wiped my face, so you must help wipe away the faults of those under your charge.

I have so much love for you that I make myself helpless in your hands. I allow you to be unfair to others, harsh to your family, impatient to your neighbor; and what you do to them you do to me. How careful this should make you in your attitude and relations toward all others!

Since the members of my Mystical Body are in a mystical way one with me, you must see me in your fellow men, not physically but with the eyes of faith. See me in the faces of little children, in the toughened hands of laborers and housewives, in the bent bodies of the aged, in the wealthy businessman and the ragged beggar. Do even more; adore me in your fellow men, even those who abuse you, adoring not the creature but me in the creature. How can you truly and fully adore me, unless you adore me also present in the members of my Mystical Body?

When you see a crippled [man] sitting on a corner selling pencils, do you say to yourself, "In him, I see Christ suffering"?

When you give blood to the Red Cross, do you realize that you give it to me? Do you think, as the needle pierces your finger that this is akin to the nails that pierced my hands? As the blood flows from your arms, do you unite it with the blood that flowed from my body on that Good Friday?

Because I abide in the members of my Mystical Body, I give you golden opportunity to serve me in all men. When you so much as feed a baby or hold it lovingly, you feed me and hold me lovingly, even as did my Mother. Thus I enable you to repay me a little for what I have done for you. Thus I make our love and our service both yours and mine.

Any work of mercy done out of love for me is priceless; and the works of mercy are far broader than help extended to the needy. Taking a friend to lunch, sharing a cake or cookie, fixing a cold drink for your family on a warm day, lending a coat or dress, taking in visitors or tourists, instructing and counseling those who question you, giving directions to a stranger, breathing a prayer for the bus driver, blessing inwardly all whom you pass on the way, sending a petition aloft when you hear the wail of an ambulance, fire engine, or police siren—all these, done out of love for me, are works of mercy without price.

Would you love me in your fellow men? Then say to me, and with me, this prayer:

> Dear Lord, may I always remember: Whatever I do to them, I do also to you.
>
> May I never forsake your command, "Love one another as I have loved you."
>
> May my thoughts of others be no longer my thoughts but your thoughts.
>
> May my love of others be no longer my love, but yours.
>
> In my speech with others may my words be no longer my words, but your words.
>
> May I serve others as you served all men, seeking not to receive but to give.
>
> May I see others no longer, but you in them.
>
> May your thoughts dwell in my mind, your love in my heart, your words on my lips—that I may learn to love all men even as you, dear Lord, love me.

Christ in Myself

> I will remain united with you.
>
> JOHN 15:4

If you try earnestly and prayerfully to imitate me, I promise you that you shall advance wonderfully in the supernatural life. Just as husbands and wives sometimes acquire each other's mannerisms and expressions, so I desire you to live in such intimacy with me that you will acquire my characteristics, my virtues, my way of living. Live thus, and I promise you that not only shall your will and mine be one, but even our thoughts and our inmost feelings shall be the same. I will live in you in a special way. You shall worship the Father with my love, look up to him with my eyes, speak to him with my works.

What a glorious privilege, to worship God with God's own love, in God's own way.

No longer shall your life be one of imitation of mine; it shall become identified with mine. Then shall you be able to say with the Apostle Paul, "It is now no longer I who live, but Christ lives in me."[10]

Think well on these truths, my chosen one. They are good tidings of great joy. Truly I call you to a life of identification with me. I, the Word of God made man, desire to praise my Father, and love him, by means of all creation.

I praise and love him not only through my Godhead but also through my manhood.

But the thirty-some years of my life on earth did not satisfy the love of my human nature for my Father. I desire to live on in you, to extend my life through yours, to love my Father in you and through you, and in and through all men for eternity.

This is why I have united myself with you in a real, but mystical way, the unity of my Mystical Body. This is why I have called you not only to imitate me, but to live in me, and I in you, so that we may be identified one with the other.

While I am moved primarily by love for my Father, I am moved also by love for you. I want you to have the glorious privilege of loving the Father through me and of letting me love him through you.

From all eternity I planned this privilege for you.

And on Calvary I gave you divine life, making you a sharer in my divine nature. There I enabled you to glorify the Father in me; there I joined you to myself in the Mystical Body; there I made you a sharer in my Sonship toward the Father. Think of him no longer as if he were your Father. Realize now that he *is* your Father in very truth.

Do you comprehend faintly what I am saying to you? I am telling you that you have God for your Father, not merely because he made you and sustains you, but because his own divine life is within you. He adds to the love. He has for you as one of his creatures the love that a Father-God has for his own child.

Furthermore, I am telling you, my other self, that I myself have need of you. I desire your body, your emotions, your thoughts, your words, your actions.

Give me your heart that together we may love the Father ardently. Give me your lips that together we may sing his praises. Give me your mind, your eyes, your hands, your entire being. In you and by you I wish to live, as it were, a second life wholly of love, which will be the complement and continuation of my earthly life in Palestine. Give all of yourself to me that through you I may give all to him. Together we shall offer the Perfect Gift; we shall give God to God.

Live my life. Be pure, so that I may be pure in you.
Be generous, so that I may be generous in you. Be diligent, zealous, temperate; be on fire with love that I
may be on fire within you.

The wondrous destiny that is yours, my other self!
The selflessness that shall lead you to be absorbed in
me! The souls that you shall save by your love! The
sinners that you shall bring to the Father by your repa-
rations! The ignorant that you shall instruct and convert through your prayers!

The desires that you shall have in your inmost
heart! The yearnings to be with me and to see the Face
of God!

Be one with me! Live my life in all that you do and
all that you experience.

Be one with me! Live my life in sickness or health,
in prosperity or depression, in peace or war.

Be one with me! Live my life in consolation or aridity, in temptation and doubt, in contempt or praise.

Live my life in all things. Say to me, "Lord, dear
Lord, I desire only your desires. I have no will but
Thine."

Live my life! If you truly love me, you will not
begrudge your work for me, nor the time and activity I
ask.

Live my life! If you truly love me, you will not
refuse to suffer, for that would be refusing to love. Do
not merely accept suffering; try to love it, as a means
of showing your devotion.

Live my life! Never, I promise, will I try you too
hard. If the bridge builder knows how much the bridge

can bear, do I not know far better the burdens you can carry?

Live my life! I will lead you and guide you, instruct you and direct you along the way, counsel you and keep my eyes fixed upon you.

Live my life! You shall be glad in the Lord; jubilant, as befits the upright of heart.

Be one with me! Be my other self! Live my life!

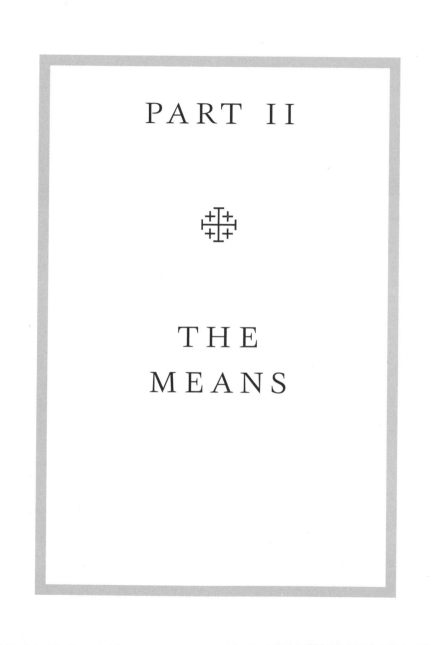

PART II

THE
MEANS

chapter five

DETACHMENT

Self-Mastery: Conquering Self

> What does it profit a man . . . ?
>
> MARK 8:36

My chosen one, realize your unbelievably good fortune. I have indeed invited you to be not merely another Christ but to be my other self.

You want to be my other self, but you also want to pamper your passions and animal appetites. You cannot do both. You cannot be my other self, unless you put off yourself.

My love can live alongside other loves as long as they are not contrary to my love and my love is supreme. Indeed I command you to love one another as I have loved you. But no contrary love, whether of person or of thing, must be allowed to supplant your love for me. You must control and conquer all desires that do lead you away from me.

It is not possible for you to be vain, loving flattery, wishing to set yourself above others and still be my other self.

It is not possible for you to-be overly sensitive, vindictive, full of controversy, in love with your own opinions, and be my other self.

You cannot be covetous, lustful, gluttonous, full of envy, and be my other self.

All these are forms of self-worship. Renounce them, purge yourself of them. And let there be no half measures.

I have said: "If your right eye tempts you to sin, pluck it out and throw it away."[1] Strive to let nothing obstruct your devotion and attachment to me, your identification with me.

To be united fully to the Blessed Trinity and to enjoy the Beatific Vision, you must be perfect. The essence of perfection is the union of your will with mine. But how can you unite your will completely with mine, unless you first conquer self-will? This is why you must uproot passion; burn out your attachment to material things; suppress the desire for praise, ease, and popularity; and conquer pride in your ideas, talents, or spiritual progress.

No unclean soul can see God. To be clean is to give yourself wholly to my will, holding nothing back. To be clean of eye and heart is to be pure of the desire for all earthly goods that are contrary to my will.

If you fail to cleanse yourself thoroughly in this life, it can only be done in purgatory. There you will be purged of self-attachment by the method of deprivation. You will be deprived of what you most ardently desire: to see me face to face. Purgatory purges because you are so near to me and yet I am beyond your reach.

How much better it is, then, to sever yourself here and now from all desires which do not lead you closer to me, not only desires which are mortally sinful but those also that are venial faults or only imperfections. All such voluntary desires serve only to weary and torment you, to blind you, to make you lukewarm. Purge yourself of these voluntary desires by denying yourself the objects and pleasures that feed them.

Seek after that which is hard, rather than that which is easy—for my love.

Seek after that which is unpleasant, rather than that which is pleasant—for my love.

Seek after that which is little, rather than that which is great—for my love.

Seek to desire nothing but what I send you, and refuse nothing that I permit to happen to you—for my love.

Are these harsh words? Do they mean that you are henceforth to give up all pleasure?

By no means! I shall guide you to the degree of self-renunciation that is best for you. What is suited to one is not to another. If you strive to do all that I ask for love you will find joy in sacrifice.

Mortify yourself; but understand that the greatest mortification is the practice of true humility. Humbly accepting the mortifications I send you is better than piling upon yourself the mortifications you choose.

Be strict in observing the fasts and penances enjoined by my Church. But remember that ordinarily I do not desire souls to take upon themselves voluntary mortifications which cause them to be irritable and discontented. Let your voluntary penances be confined to those which do not disturb your peace of mind. It is possible to be a slave to mortification.

From time to time I send you suffering. I want to make you mine more fully by severing the earthly attachments that separate us. Will the sufferings that I send you and your burden shall become light, because my yoke is easy for those who love me.

The desire to suffer for my sake is holy; but even better is the virtue of indifference. Seek to do my will in joy or sorrow with holy indifference, saying in your deepest soul that you choose neither pleasure nor pain and that you desire only what conforms to my will. Strive to love me equally in all things: in sickness or health, life or death, wealth or poverty, pleasure or pain, consolations or desolations.

Do not become unduly attached even to perfection. Since you cannot, now, serve me perfectly, offer to me your discontent with yourself. Desire nothing more at this moment than to serve me as best you can. Let your only aim be to please me in the way I give you.

Beware, in short, lest you become a slave to anything of earth, but especially to pleasure. I know full well that the human body and mind need relaxation. What you do to yourself, you do to me. When you delight in healthy pleasure, I share your delight, for I am with you and in you. But seek no pleasure except such that I can partake of with you. Seek it at such time as I can approve. Seek it in such degree as I would wish. Ask yourself from time to time in the midst of your pleasures, "Could I give this up at once if I knew it to be God's will? Can I leave this, here and now, without being distressed?"

To be completely my other self you must be wholly mine, desiring to do only my will. The "purer" you are, the "cleaner" your heart, the more fully I shall dwell within you.

The Secret: Attachment

> Put on the new self. . . .
>
> EPHESIANS 4:24

Now I shall tell you a great principle. Strive less for de-tachment than for at-tachment. Concentrate more on filling yourself with what *is* me, than on emptying yourself of what is *not* me. Allow me to come into your soul and I will push out of it what is alien to me. Let me flood your soul with grace, washing away the unclean bonds of worldliness. This is the peaceful way to purity of heart, the quiet, easy, trusting way, the way of a little child.

You have many natural tendencies to conquer. But one always predominates. What is your ruling pleasure or passion? Perhaps you do not know. Ask me, and I shall help you discover it.

What most upsets you? What do you worry about? What is the love, the desire, above all others, that you find hardest to submit to my will? Is it impurity? bad companions? inordinate pride? Is it the love of money? the desire for prestige? Is it gossip? impatience?

You can tell the desires to which you are attached by the things which irritate you. If you frequently become irritated when you are bothered while reading the paper, you are attached to privacy or to your enjoyment of the paper. If you become irritated when contradicted, you are attached to "being right." If you feel envious when others are promoted, you are attached to the desire for prestige, advancement, or money. If you feel uncomfortable when another gets a choice bit of meat or a larger dessert than you, you are attached to the pleasures of food.

Examine yourself earnestly, and pray to me for guidance; I will reveal to you the key defect that stands in the way of your identification with me.

Once you have discovered it, replace it with its contrary virtue.

Study in me the virtue that is directly opposed to your predominant vice. Go to Scripture to see how I practiced it; note the circumstances as they are described in the Gospels.

Are you proud? Study my humility and *attach* it to yourself.

Are you covetous? Study my generosity and *attach* it to yourself.

Are you envious? Study my benevolence and *attach* it to yourself.

Are you intemperate in food and drink? Study my temperance and *attach* it to yourself.

Are you given to anger? Study my patience and *attach* it to yourself.

Are you lustful? Study my purity and *attach* it to yourself.

Are you lazy? Do you spend too much time in recreation, in sleep, in reading, watching television, and conversing? Study my diligence and *attach* it to yourself.

Plan to practice the virtue that you need most. Visualize the precise circumstances you are likely to encounter this day in which you will be able to put on this virtue. Talk over your plan with me. Call to mind your resolution from time to time during the day.

When you are tempted, and even when you fall, do not be dismayed. Concentrate on how you will practice this virtue in similar circumstances in the future. Turn to me. Recall the way I practiced this virtue, and breathe a prayer, "Lord, help me; Jesus, teach me; Master, strengthen me."

In all things, seek my aid and you shall find it. Ask my Mother to give you her hand, and she will never refuse.

Say to me now this prayer of attachment:

Dear Lord, I offer you my very life, and I willingly
accept all the joys and sorrows it may contain.

I offer you my worldly goods; if it be your will
that I should lose my possessions, this is also
my will.

I offer you my family and friends, accepting here
and now the hour and circumstances of my
parting from them.

I offer you my death with all the pains that may
surround it. I desire neither to lengthen nor to
shorten my life by a single moment.

I offer you the sufferings of those I love, sufferings often harder for me to bear than my own.

I offer you all the disappointment, injustices,
heartaches, that will come to my dear ones, in
union with Mary offering your sufferings on
the cross.

Help me, dear Christ, to put off self. Fill me with
your virtues. Make your will my will.

You ask of me the greatest gift I can give: myself.
But you return to me the greatest gift God can
give: yourself.

Help me, dear Master, to be generous, unselfish,
persevering.

Transform me into yourself. As the priest
changes bread and wine into your Body and
Blood, change me into an extension of yourself, another Christ, your other self.

The Spirit of Poverty

> Blessed are the poor in spirit. . . .
> MATTHEW 5:3 (KNOX TRANSLATION)

My chosen one, I would have your heart free of the desire for worldly goods.

It is poverty of spirit, not actual poverty of possessions, that is essential. Not money, but the love of money, is the root of evil; not wealth, but the craving for it, damages the soul. Wealth is outside of you, your desires are within; and it is from within the heart of man that evils come. Yet you must beware lest the possession of riches breed covetousness in your soul.

Where your treasure house is, there your heart is also. Therefore, do not greedily seek to lay up treasures on earth, but let your heart calmly rest in me.

Only if you do this can you live in peace and serenity. There is no peace in the greedy pursuit of material things.

Do not be too anxious over your life, how you will support it with food and drink and clothing. Life itself is a greater gift than food or clothing. Your Father has given you life and he will provide. He feeds the birds of the air who never sow or reap. Are you dearer to him than they?

It is for the heathens to busy themselves with material things; you have a Father in heaven who knows what you need. Seek first the kingdom of God, and his will, and all the material things you need shall be yours.

It is not my will that all should be actually poor; it is my will that all should be poor in spirit. It is possible to be poor in things, yet proud in spirit. On the other hand, you may be rich as a king in possessions, yet truly poor in spirit. Or you may be neither rich nor poor, yet practice poverty of spirit.

I have shown you by my example how to practice Christian poverty in whatever condition of life you may be.

I, the Son of God, came into the world possessing nothing; no house, no crib. A rude cave and a manger and swaddling clothes were my nursery. As an infant I had to flee with Mary and Joseph from my homeland to Egypt because Herod sought to kill me.

I left the world on the cross still possessing nothing. My clothing was stripped from my body and the soldiers drew lots for my robe. Not even the cross, the bed upon which I died, was mine, nor the nails that held my feet.

They offered me a sedative, wine mixed with gall; but I refused to possess even this.

To fulfill ancient prophecies I was reckoned among the wicked. I died, not amid the tears and sorrow of my people, but amid their jeers. My good name was stolen from me. They taunted me, "Save yourself and come down from the cross. . . . Let the messias, the king of the Jews, come down from the cross this instant."[2] Abandoned by nearly all of my dearest friends, I suffered the more because my Mother witnessed my grievous torments.

If you are poor, remember that I was poorer a thousand times.

Follow my example. Accept your poverty of the present moment as coming from the Father, even as I accepted mine. Do not complain, but do not hesitate to ask the Father for aid to bear your cross and your sufferings.

If you are truly poor, regard it as a great blessing. I would not allow you to be so unless it were best, nor permit you to remain so without giving you grace to turn it to your eternal joy. Accept your present poverty with a simple and pure resignation. The poverty that comes to you from my will is no less an opportunity for love than that which you might voluntarily take on yourself.

It may be more difficult by far to accept the humiliation of actual poverty than to be content with voluntary poverty, which is often salved by the admiration and respect of your fellow men.

Do not shrink from this cross, this privilege, of poverty. Unite it to my will; offer it to the Father. Do not be too proud to accept charity, nor to beg it if necessary. Give others opportunity to serve me through you, remembering that whatever they do for you, my poor one, they do also for me. Give me through your humility the privilege of being served by them as I so ardently desire. Your poverty may be the means of their eternal salvation.

The Right Use of Wealth

> Make use of your base wealth. . . .
>
> LUKE 16:9 (KNOX)

If you are rich, I was richer a thousand times.

Is not all the world mine, and everything that is in it?

What man has ever enjoyed the beauties of creation as I have done? What monarch can command the wind and the waves, multiply loaves and fishes, heal the sick, give sight to the blind, raise the dead?

What riches, what powers, are there that were not mine to use? Even on the cross I could give the good thief Paradise.

Are there delights or is there knowledge in the world that I did not possess? From the moment of my conception in my Mother's womb I enjoyed the Beatific Vision. My Mother was the fairest of all creatures, the Queen of heaven and earth.

Learn of me, you who are wealthy. Make your goods your servants; never let them become your masters. Be ever alert, lest you become too attached to wealth. Do you take pride in your possessions? Do you worry about your goods, think about them constantly? If you do, beware. Are you terribly troubled when you lose some of your possessions? Examine your heart to learn where your affections lie.

I did not hoard my riches. I used them generously for the health, happiness, and welfare of my fellow men. So you, too, should often give of your wealth to the truly poor. Deprive yourself. Make sacrifices. Thus you will be master of your possessions, and you will be free from affection for them.

Do even more than this. Love the poor. Seek them out. Invite them to your home. Go to them in theirs. And if you would be perfect in the spirit of poverty, do not hesitate to make yourself the servant of the poor. Louis of France served the poor at his own table. With his own hands he changed their bandages. Here was a king who was truly poor in spirit. Elizabeth, princess of Hungary, also practiced spiritual poverty in visiting the poor.

All this was in imitation of me, because I surrounded myself with the poor and unfortunate. When the disciples of John the Baptist came to me with their question, did I not explain that the poor have the Gospel preached to them?

Though rich, you may yet practice poverty in all these ways. Indeed, you may often practice even a semblance of actual poverty, for it must frequently happen that you lack this or that possession when you most desire it. You are giving a dinner and the service is inadequate; you are embarrassed before your guests. Calmly accept this semblance of poverty. You are driving on the highway and your car breaks down. Accept this inconvenience in peace. You are stranded by the weather in a city far from your destination. Keep your serenity. You are guilty of clumsiness or of involuntarily offending good taste. Accept your humiliation. This, too, is poverty and must be received with true poverty of spirit.

Perhaps you are neither rich nor poor and therefore unable to practice the poverty of either the beggar or the king. Still you must be poor in spirit, and I have shown you how. Use the worldly goods you have and need, but never let your heart rest in them.

Do you recall how I used the boats of my Apostles when I had need of them; how I visited at Peter's house in Capharnaum and with my friends Mary, Martha, and Lazarus in Bethany, and with Zaccheus, the chief publican, in Jericho? But when such possessions were not needed or were not at hand and I had no place to lay my head, that, too, was equally acceptable to me.

I fasted for forty days; yet I banqueted with Matthew and his friends and with Simon the leper. I attended the marriage feast of Cana and dined with Simon the Pharisee. The Pharisees called me a glutton because I feasted with those I came to save.

Do you see the lesson I would teach you? Be indifferent to your worldly goods, yet use them wisely. Do not wish too eagerly to acquire more than you have. Do not let your heart be captured by affection for the goods you possess.

Care for your possessions reasonably, knowing that all things are mine and that you are my steward. In a serene and peaceable spirit, seek not only to preserve but even to increase your possessions so long as you may do so justly and in keeping with your state of life. Be wary, however, of the love of things, which is really self-love; and do not hesitate to part with your possessions for the good of your neighbor.

Give according to your means, whatever your station in life may be. The less of wealth you have to give, the more I would have you offer other gifts that you do possess. Do you recall how Peter said to the lame beggar: "Silver and gold I have none; but what I have, that I give you,"[3] and in my name he gave back to him the use of his limbs?

Give what you have to your neighbor, which is to give it to me. Give your prayers, your cheerfulness of disposition, your smile, your kindness, your consolation, your sympathy. Give a "God bless you," a pat on the back, a glad "good-morning." Keep nothing back. Give generously of all that you possess according to your ability.

Thus you will practice true Christian poverty, and I shall say to you one day with infinite love, "Come, my other self; blessed are you who are poor in spirit; yours is the kingdom of heaven."

The Widow's Mite

> She . . . put in all she possessed, yes, all she had to live on.
>
> MARK 12:44

One day when my disciples and I were watching the rich throw money into the temple treasury, a poor widow came and put in two little coins. And I said, ". . . this widow, the beggar woman that she is, has put in more than all the others that put money into the treasury: all the others took from their superfluities what they put in; but this woman, in her extreme want, put in all she possessed, yes, all she had to live on."[4]

What does this incident teach? It teaches that the gift is far less important than the spirit of the giving.

If you lovingly give me your all, no matter how small, it is worth more in my eyes than the giving of much by those who have much but still keep something back.

Your "widow's mite," my other self, is not only money, it is all the material, spiritual, mental, and social goods that you possess. Give them all to me. Be ready to offer me everything you have, even your loved ones and your peace of mind, if such be my will.

With the help of my grace, such poverty of spirit is possible. At the divine command, Abraham was ready to sacrifice Isaac, his only son. Job suffered the loss of his wealth, his health, his children; yet he did not turn from his Maker. My sorrowful Mother watched me die on the cross, but no complaining word passed her lips.

Just as they allowed nothing to stand in the way of the divine will, so you, if you would be completely my other self, must strip yourself of all attachments which separate us.

If you realize the truth that nothing is yours, you will find this detachment easier.

Even your good thoughts do not belong to you but to the Holy Spirit.

Nothing is yours: no spiritual goods, no consolation, no holy desire, no prayer. They are all my gifts. If I choose to give you consolations to lead you to my side, be grateful; but do not seek them or become attached to them. If I choose to give you desolation, stripping you of earthly desires and affections and leading you through the dark nights of the senses and the spirit to closer union with me, be more thankful still. The dark nights are a far greater blessing than consolation, because they are the safe road for my chosen ones to intimate union with me. Do not be alarmed or discouraged. Give yourself to me completely; say to me that you do my will not because it gives you joy but solely because you love me.

If nothing is yours, then you yourself are not yours. Although you know that you belong to your Maker, you frequently act as if you alone were the source of all your talents and abilities. You act as if you were your own.

Meditate on the truth that you are my creature, utterly mine. If you do this, you will suddenly find the warmest consolation in the knowledge that you belong to the all-good, the all-powerful, all-loving God. Since you belong to him, he will surely care for you with surpassing tenderness. How wonderful, how peaceful, to belong to God. Can you imagine anything better?

Cling to nothing but me. Hoard no thing, not even your good name. Blessed are you when men revile you, and persecute you, and speak evil against you falsely because of me. Be lighthearted to be stripped thus of your possessions.

Are you glad, my other self, when you are reviled and persecuted because of me? Or are you indignant and rebellious? It is good to stand up for truth and to oppose those who obstruct the coming of the kingdom of God. But be careful that your zeal be truly for my kingdom.

Learn to love my will.

You are not only to accept whatever I send you; you are to love the will that sends it.

When you truly love my will, you will be almost completely unconcerned about what happens to you, so long as it happens by my design. Many of my saints arrived at a state of almost complete indifference, desiring nothing, refusing nothing, requesting nothing except the grace to know and to do my will. Thérèse, in her prayer of oblation, asked that she reach the position in heaven I had destined for her. She was not curious as to whether it should be relatively high or low. My will was her sole desire, because she loved my will.

Imitate her, my other self. Then you will accept with equal love desolation or consolation, rain or sunshine, poverty or wealth. You will look calmly to the future. You will think and pray in your deepest heart, "Your will, whatever it is—and I do not care unduly to know—be done."

Do this, and possess my peace.

Christ Wants Our All

> He bore our sins in his own body. . . .
>
> 1 PETER 2:24

Do not be overly curious about your progress in the spiritual life. As long as you are faithful to my grace, I will fit your growth to your capacity. Commit the progress of your spiritual life to me. Say to me, "Into your hands, Lord, I place my past, my present, my future."

How inexorable is the progress I demand of you! Yet how tenderly I lead you. You have so much to learn, and so many worldly desires to unlearn. You must learn to punish yourself by fasting and mortification in the things of sense. You must learn to accept peacefully the mortifications that are sent to you, especially those which flow from your state of life. You must learn to practice interior mortifications: biting back to the desire to boast, to glory in your successes, to take pride in your natural talents. You must learn to treasure the spiritual mortifications that come to you: desolation and aridity, unjust accusations, misunderstanding of your motives and good intentions.

You must learn to prize injustices and deprivations to your dear ones, especially your family. How difficult it is for a mother and father to endure injury and injustice to their children, knowing that they are helpless to defend themselves.

But you are not the first to undergo these torments, my other self. Was it easy for my Mother to bring me into the world in a cave that served as a stable? Was it easy for her to flee with me from the murderous wrath of Herod? Was it easy to meet me on the way to the cross, to stand beneath the gibbet watching my life's blood trickle down into the thirsty earth, to hold my lifeless Body in her arms when the cross finally released me, to place me in the tomb?

Do you think that the events of her life were easier for her to bear because she knew how they would turn out? No, she did not know what dangers would be encountered in Egypt, nor when Joseph would die, nor how I would be received by those I came to save. She did not know how much I must suffer. She knew only that the Father watches over all and she united her will with his.

Mary accepted my sorrows because she loved the will of God. I accepted her sorrows because this was the will of my Father, and I love his will.

So, too, you must grasp, and with eager hands, the mortifications that come to you through your dear ones. Parents must protect their children from harm; but they must also teach them to value affronts, to brave humiliations, to treasure pain; and they must themselves clasp to their bosoms the hardship that a child's pain inflicts upon a loving parental heart, even as Mary held her dolors close to her soul. There is hardly any lesson more difficult to learn and practice than this.

As you advance in my way, you will offer me more and more. You will offer me your acceptance of your present situation and of whatever the future may bring. You will offer me your own death, your acceptance of purgatory and of whatever place in my heavenly court I have destined for you.

So selfless shall you be that you will begin to pray that the whole world may love me even more than you do, and serve me better. You know well that you love me; and in this prayer you will make yourself "least" in my kingdom. This will be your desire: that you may be the least of all men, that you may have your place on the edge of heaven, so to speak, because then you will know that I must indeed be well loved by all of my creatures. Thus you will think not of yourself but only of me; not of how devout you are, but of how devoted to me all should be; not of how much you do, but of how much should be done in my service.

And all this will please me beyond reckoning.

But unless I remind you, you will forget to offer one thing, and that is your sins.

You must give me everything, my other self. If you refuse to give me your sins, how can I feel free to give you the trials and tests you need to learn truly to love my will? Give me your sins, and I shall feel free to confer upon you the sufferings you need. But if you hold back your sins and if you say to me: "No, dear Lord, it is unfair. I cannot do this to you," then I must feel your lack of confidence in me, I shall be reluctant to send you the pains you sorely need, because you also might say to me, "Lord, it is unfair."

Much as I told Peter when he refused to allow me to wash his feet, so I now tell you: unless I do this, you cannot have companionship with me. Unless you let me take your faults and sins, you cannot be my other self.

Will you not say to me:

Take my sins, dearest Lord, as you desire, and
     give to me trials and sufferings. Take my
     impurities, my quarreling, my disobedience,

my laziness, my unkindness, my impatience,
my disrespect, my thefts, my lies, my angers,
my intemperance, my avarice, my horrible
pride.

Take all these sins and faults and cleanse my soul
with a single drop of your precious Blood—
and teach me to love your will.

I am yours, Lord, and I belong to none but you; I
love you more than my own being, more than
myself. I am not my own, I am wholly yours,
your other self.

Thus you will be poor in spirit, but incomparably
rich in me; you will be detached from worldly goods,
but inextricably attached to me; you will own nothing,
but possess everything.

chapter six

VIRTUE

Humility

> Be of the same mind as Christ Jesus. . . .
>
> PHILIPPIANS 2:5

Had you been at the Last Supper, my other self, you would have learned two lessons. You would have learned love: "A new commandment I give you: love one another; as I love you, so I want you, too, to love one another."[1]

And you would have learned humility: I would have washed your feet.

Humility does not consist in outward acts, though acts are motivated by it. Humility is within. It is an interior disposition to know the truth about yourself, to accept it, and to live according to it. It is the solid base upon which you must build your spiritual life.

The humility of my saints has never failed to endear them to the Trinity. Learn humility from Mary. She, the Mother of the Most High, the most favored of my creatures, was not puffed up. She recognized, accepted, and lived the truth about herself, doing perfectly the task given her. Though she knew she was blessed above all women upon the earth, she did not retire into privacy, waiting for the world to recognize her pre-eminence and come to serve her. Hearing that Elizabeth, her cousin, is in her sixth month, she straightway goes to her and stays for three months. Then with superb consideration, she departs; Elizabeth should enjoy the son of her old age and be queen of her house. Nothing should interfere. Having served her cousin, Mary quietly effaces herself.

Humility!

My Virgin Mother, far surpassing Joseph in grace and dignity, submitted to him in all things concerning the headship of the family, as fitted her earthly station in life. It was to Joseph that the angel appeared when it became necessary to fly into Egypt. It was to Joseph that the angel brought the news of Herod's death and the message that it was now safe to return to Palestine. And Mary obeyed Joseph, unquestioning, though her dignity surpassed that of all the angels.

Learn humility also from John the Baptist, than whom there was no greater prophet among the sons of women. Study his self-effacement in not leaving the Jordan to seek me out and in not physically following me once he discovered me. "One has to be content," said John, "with what has been assigned him by heaven."[2] So John remained on the Jordan and did his tasks until the day Herod threw him into prison for speaking God's truth.

Learn humility, my other self, from the Son of Man, who as a Child obeyed his own creatures; who said to John in his baptism, let us "fulfill, as is proper for us, all just demands."[3] He paid the temple pence so that no one would be scandalized, and his lips again and again uttered the phrase of obedience: that the Scriptures might be fulfilled.

I chose to become a human being, a servant, a creature, claiming no special immunities from the lot of mankind, to live on earth amid the pains and penalties brought into the world by sin. Having made this choice, and fully knowing what it entailed, my human will never once murmured, much less rebelled, against the wrongs, injustices, and torments that befell me.

I submitted to all things from my creatures. They insulted me, called me insane, scorned me as the vilest of beings, a devil. They arrested me, imprisoned me, beat me, mocked me, and spat upon me. How would you respond to such outrages from creatures of yours, whose lives you held in the palm of your hand, creatures who could neither move nor exist without your will?

They pounded nails through my wrists and feet. They left me hanging from two timbers, slowly choking to death, while my Mother watched at my feet. Would you submit to this from your own creatures?

It was my Father's will that I should suffer and therefore it was my will.

Adam and Eve had only to obey; despite all the advantages they possessed, they would not admit the supremacy of their Creator.

I atoned for their sin by obeying completely in all things, though the devil hurled all his fury against me. Attacked in the garden by the agonizing thoughts of the day just ahead, overwhelmed by bearing upon my shoulders all the sins of mankind, having allowed myself to be given over to the terrifying temptation to refuse to suffer this most awful of torments, I submitted completely. "May your will, not mine, be done."[4] This is humility, my other self. Learn of me!

Christ: The Model

> Learn from me; I am gentle and humble
> of heart.
>
> Matthew 11:29 (Knox)

Perhaps you think that I cannot truly be your model in humility, because, being God, I am omnipotent. How wrong you are if this is your thought. Did I call on my divinity in Bethlehem to provide shelter or comfort for the Holy Family? When Herod sought my life, did I save myself through omnipotence? Joseph and Mary fled with me on the long, hard journey exactly as any other parents with a child would have had to do.

Did I make my boyhood easy with miracles? None of my associates in Nazareth saw me as other than the son of Joseph and Mary. My cousins, hearing of my public teaching, thought me beside myself.

When I was famished after fasting forty days in the desert and was tempted by Satan to make bread of stones, did I lightly use my omnipotence to serve myself? When I was thirsty, did I not ask for water at Jacob's well as any man might have done? And when I miraculously multiplied the loaves and fishes was it not to feed others, not myself? When I was fatigued, I slept; when Lazarus died, I wept; and when I was maligned and misunderstood, I was sad, even as you.

Study my miracles and you will see that they were done to help the needy and to prove my divinity that men might believe in me and be saved. Never did I use my supernatural power to serve myself; always it was to carry out the eternal designs of my Father.

When my enemies sought me, I remained away from Jerusalem, using the natural means of safety available to all men. And when finally my time had come, I freely delivered myself into their hands. Though I could have freed myself by a mere thought, I permitted myself to be condemned to death by one of my creatures. Though I might have prevented it with a single glance, I allowed myself to be scourged mercilessly and crowned with thorns. I bore my cross, falling beneath it and rising again, accepting the aid of Simon's strong hands and Veronica's pitying ministrations, but doing nothing of myself to ease my agony. I refused the sedative offered me, that not one pain should be lessened. On the cross I forgave the thief in another manifestation of my divinity; but I would not come down from my bed of torment.

Yes, my other self, I can be your Model. I *am* your Model.

Now let us apply this to your life. For you, even as for me, the Father uttered his eternal word, a "word" containing all that your life should be. Your duty, like mine, so far as my humanity is concerned, is to live as the Father's word ordains, desiring nothing else, refusing naught of sorrow or joy that it contains, giving yourself lovingly to its fulfillment. This word is my Father's plan for every detail of your life, for your place in eternity. You are a piece in the wondrous jigsaw of the eternal plan.

As I united my will to the word uttered by my Father for my life on earth, so you must unite your will with his word for your life. Since the world is full of sin and sinners, your life, too, will contain monotony, fatigue, injustices, insults, offenses against your person, perhaps even persecution and death. Accept it, all of it. Say to my Father: "Behold your servant, O Lord. Be it done according to your word." Do not rebel against your Creator who does not will these things, but permits them to happen only because he has given men freedom, freedom to love and freedom to hate, freedom to obey and freedom to sin. To rebel is to refuse to recognize that you are a sinner and the world is a world of sin. It is to resent that your fellow men are free. It is to refuse to recognize your position as my creature. It is to abjure humility and welcome pride.

I do not tell you to be passive in the face of evil. Your duty is to remedy such conditions so far as you reasonably can. But while you seek remedies, do not complain, much less rebel, against my divine providence.

To be humble, you must see and accept yourself as you truly are: created out of nothing, held in existence only by my will, depending entirely on me, capable of nothing supernaturally good except through me.

Yet this is not all. Though you are a sinner, you have been redeemed by me. You are an heir of the Eternal Majesty, a child of God, another Christ, beloved of my Father even as I am beloved of him. What a joy it should be to know that my Father loves you as he loves me.

This is the truth. And because I am "the Truth" can you not see how I must love humility, and how I must hate pride? Pride is a lie and a theft; it usurps my divine rights. It seeks to subordinate your God to one of his creatures. I cannot cease to be God, cede to you my divine prerogatives, substitute your plan of creation for mine.

How I hate pride, the capital vice, the sin of Lucifer, the sin of Adam and Eve which brought discord and suffering into the world. It is pride which sows the seed of complete disunity between God and man, which slams the door in the face of my divine grace, which in a sense makes null and void my bitter passion and cruel death.

Because I am God, I must resist the proud and exalt the humble.

Progress in Humility

> I take delight, for Christ's sake, in infirmities. . . .
> 2 CORINTHIANS 12:10

Are you humble?

Let us see. Do you delight in talking about yourself either in self-praise or self-blame? Are you a "show-off," a monopolizer of conversation? Are you argumentative, easily angered, sarcastic, given to ridicule? Do you brood over your humiliations and refuse to take correction, excusing yourself and blaming others when things go wrong? Do you complain about the way people treat you, sulk when you lose at games, disparage others when they win favors? Do you find it hard to obey your superiors? Do you refuse to obey your equals or inferiors?

Having some of these defects does not mean necessarily that you are proud. They may stem from a childish desire to be one of the crowd or from feelings of inferiority. Nevertheless, they are danger signs.

Examine yourself. Admit your faults. Then ask my help and I will allow you to draw from the limitless treasure of my virtues.

You need my help. Ask it! My desire is to give, and to give abundantly, full measure, pressed down and running over.

Do you desire humility? Ask me. Purity? Ask me. Faith? Ask me. Trust? Ask me. Love? Ask me. Holiness? Ask me. You will make more progress in a moment of fervent prayer for a share in my virtues than in a lifetime of your own striving.

Pray for humility and I will take you at your word. You will begin to find yourself being misunderstood, passed over, rebuked, perhaps ridiculed. When this happens try to remember to thank me for giving you these precious opportunities to practice meekness, to choke back harsh and indignant words, to refrain from expressing unnecessarily your own opinions or to challenge the opinions others advance.

These will be hard lessons and, at times, bitter ones. To be humble will be difficult as you try to control the temptation to be sharp or cross with others. But I am ready always to help you lift yourself to me and tell me that you want these lessons, that you would not forego them, that you will them because you know I am teaching you and my teaching is perfect.

And suddenly, for no apparent reason, the pressure will ease. You will find, for a time at least, that it has become rather simple to speak little of yourself, to avoid curiosity, to accept correction, not to parade your talents.

You will even begin to accept the blame calmly for mishaps of which you are innocent, to take slights smilingly, to be serene in the midst of your clumsiness and blunders. You may be glad when you are ridiculed, rejoicing in your lowliness.

You will, of course, have alternate periods of failure and success. Very often you will feel that you are failing these lessons in humility. You may restrain your tongue, conquer the urge to refuse to do some menial task, try to put out of your mind thoughts that you are not appreciated, turn your back and leave the room to prevent your giving way to irritation; but all the while you will feel that you are not really succeeding in humbling yourself. You are holding yourself in check, but you are not humble.

And when you fall—as you will—your chagrin will be painful. But if only you continue to rise, you will finally learn a profound truth: that you should accept this disappointment itself in a new way; that you should say to yourself and to me, "I will this disappointment; I want it, because I deserve it and it is good for me. I don't like it, for it hurts, but I will it."

Once you do this, it will be as though a riddle had suddenly solved itself. You will clearly see that humility does not consist in liking humiliations, but only in willing them, in choosing them, perhaps in seeking them, but not at all in liking them.

My martyrs did not like pain. John the Baptist did not like to stay on the Jordan when he might have been with me. Joseph and Mary did not like to fly with me to Egypt. Mary did not like to stand on Calvary. I did not like to die on the cross. But the more our senses and passions said no, the more our wills said yes.

No, my other self, you need not, and you will not, like humiliations. But the more intense your dislike of them, the greater your opportunity to serve me and to redeem souls by willing them.

Remember that whatever happens to you is not too severe a penalty for your misdeeds of the past. With Francis of Assisi, nod your head on being pelted with insults and worse, always recognizing that you deserve "injustice" for not turning sooner to your God, for not serving him better, for not thanking him for his favors, for not appreciating the many pitfalls from which he has saved you, for not responding to his flood of graces. Is it not, in a sense, joy to unite your sufferings with mine? Say with Paul, "Gladly, therefore, will I boast of my infirmities, that the power of Christ may spread a sheltering cover over me. For this reason I take delight, for Christ's sake, in infirmities, in insults, in hardships, in persecutions, in distresses. For when I am weak, then I am strong."[5]

Do not, then, think as you have in the past, "I will be a fool for no one." Rather say: "Gladly will I be a fool for Christ; I will delight in being his fool, in being humiliated for him, ridiculed, scorned, persecuted, even as he was a fool for me nineteen centuries ago."

The Key to Peace of Soul

> Humble yourselves before the Lord, and he
> will exalt you.
>
> JAMES 4:10

You will make progress in humility. But even as you advance, you must beware of the insidious inroads of pride. The evil one will urge you to compare your state with that of others and to take pride even in your humility. Beware! Whatever is good in you, you owe not to yourself but to me. It is I who inspired you to good, who nurtured the thought, who smoothed the way, strengthened you against weakness, led you through obstacles, called you when you strayed, watched over you with a care and love far beyond your comprehensions. Take no glory for yourself, but give all glory to God.

I will test your humility not only through your humiliations but through those of your dear ones as well. This will be a great opportunity for you to practice humility. In these afflictions say to yourself: "If this is painful, this small humiliation to one I love, how Mary must have suffered at his degradation. Yet she never spoke a word of complaint; she never asked to be spared. She, too, was a victim of God's love."

Another stern test may be your willingness to accept with equal temper either obscurity or fame. Those whose talents are hidden by some defect and who see less intelligent persons forge ahead while they themselves are held back should offer their obscurity to me. Such a sacrifice can be even more difficult than the offering of the monk and nun who give up their place in the world to hide in monastery and convent.

Involuntary obscurity, made voluntary by an act of your will, becomes a shining sacrifice, an act of great love.

Unite your obscurity to that of Mary and Joseph. So hidden were they that Scripture does not even record when they died.

Do not shrink, then, from obscurity and humiliation. But remember also that humiliation is not itself humility. Humility, as I have told you, is the recognition of your place in my plan and your wholehearted acceptance of it. You must not put humiliation above duty, for this would be denying humility. You have a duty in charity to take reasonable care to preserve your good name, just as you have a duty to take reasonable efforts to correct error. If you are unjustly accused in a matter not wholly unimportant, it is right to deny your guilt calmly. Having adequately done so, if the accusations continue, it is then proper to say no more, and to leave your good name to my protection.

Again it is a good exercise in humility never to contradict another in matters of no importance; but it is wrong to be silent where harm or sin is involved and correction lies within your province.

Humility will be your key to peace of soul. Because I myself give you rest when you humbly and meekly take my yoke, it will be easy for you to live amid affronts or poverty, enduring the affairs of the day calmly. Being humble, you will not be ambitious, puffed up, filled with self-importance. You will have but one desire: to do the will of my Father. In activity, you will be conscious not so much of doing this or that work, but of first and always doing the will of God. That is why you will not be distressed if your work does not result successfully. Being humble, you will calmly and peacefully do your reasonable best, seeking to please your superiors who stand before you in the place of God; but you will not be disquieted if,

having done your reasonable best, your superiors are
displeased or your work ends in failure.

Say with me now this prayer:

> O Lord, so meek and humble of heart, help me to
> learn and love humility. Restrain my tongue
> when I would speak of myself. Check me when I
> would become contentious, quarrelsome, dissatis-
> fied with my lot. Help me to think as little as pos-
> sible of myself, and as much as possible of the
> Blessed Trinity and of my fellow men, in whom I
> must see you.

> O Jesus, meek and humble of heart, have mercy
>   on me.
> From the wish to be esteemed, deliver me,
>   O Jesus.
> From the wish to be loved, deliver me, O Jesus.
> From the wish to be honored, deliver me,
>   O Jesus.
> From the wish to be praised, to be preferred to
>   others, deliver me, O Jesus.
> From the desire to be asked for advice, deliver
>   me, O Jesus.
> From the desire to be approved, deliver me,
>   O Jesus.
> From the fear of being humiliated, deliver me,
>   O Jesus.
> From the fear of being despised, deliver me,
>   O Jesus.
> From the fear of being rebuked, deliver me,
>   O Jesus.

From the fear of being maligned, deliver me,
O Jesus.

From the fear of being forgotten, deliver me,
O Jesus.

From the fear of being ridiculed, deliver me,
O Jesus.

From the fear of being treated unfairly, deliver
me, O Jesus.

From the fear of being suspected, deliver me,
O Jesus.

That others be more loved than I, O Jesus, give
me the grace of this holy desire.

That others grow in the esteem of the world and
I decrease, O Jesus, give me the grace of this
holy desire.

That others be entrusted with work and I be put
aside, O Jesus, give me the grace of this holy
desire.

That others be praised and I be neglected,

O Jesus, give me the grace of this holy desire.

That others be preferred to me in all things,

O Jesus, give me the grace of this holy desire.

That others become holier than I, provided that I,
too, become as holy as I can, O Jesus, give me
the grace of this holy desire.[6]

Patience

> Be patient in tribulation. . . .
>
> ROMANS 12:12

You know, my other self, that you cannot often do magnificent things; but you can always do little everyday things magnificently. You may never have an opportunity to practice fortitude in persecution, to give to the poor all that you possess, to risk your life to save that of another, or to offer yourself as a martyr. But every day you have a hundred opportunities to be kind to your neighbor, instantly obedient to your superiors, generous to your inferiors, cheerful in your work, helpful to your family and companions, meek in your imperfections, submissive to the circumstances of the weather, uncomplaining when plans go wrong, forbearing when slighted, forgiving when wronged.

I love the practice of the virtues in little things. That is why I said in my Sermon on the Mount: "Blessed are the meek and gentle, for they will inherit the land."[7]

Hardly any virtue is so frequently tested as this. How many times daily do you have occasion to be patient with others or with circumstances not of your liking! You are in haste and people get in your way. You long for peace and quiet and others interrupt you. Your superior is cross, your inferiors are insolent, your companions slight you. Your children spill food or paw the furniture with greasy hands or mark the walls with crayons or tear up the yard with their games.

What do you do? Do you brush aside those who get in your way, shout at those who disturb you, snap back at those who criticize you?

And with what result: tension, irritation, shame-faced anger at yourself?

How much better it would be if you were patient, serene, at peace.

I will help you to learn patience.

First, pray. Again I say: In this and all your spiritual activities you will make more progress in a moment of humble prayer than in a lifetime of your own unaided striving.

Pray for the grace to see me in others with the eyes of faith. Pray for light to understand that when you are irritable with your fellow men you are irritable with me.

Surely if I could wash the feet of my disciples, you can with patience wipe up an egg that your child has broken, bear in peace a word of criticism, or hold your tongue in the face of discourtesy.

Think of my patience with your failings, forgettings, and negligences. In the "Our Father" you ask forgiveness as you forgive. Apply to your own life the parable of the merciful master and the unmerciful servant. As I forgive you what you owe and cannot or do not pay, so you should forgive others what they owe you and cannot or do not pay. Put off yourself, put on me, and patience will be yours. Do not let yourself become too attached to what you are doing or what you desire. Over-attachment leads you to be more interested in obedience, deference, quiet, or privacy for your own sake rather than for love of me. This is the result of acting from mixed motives, not from the pure love of God.

Do not ignore the faults of those whom you should rightfully correct. But be gentle; always, my other self, be gentle. Correct others for my sake, not to provide an outlet for your irritation or outraged pride. Correct in a spirit of helpfulness, not of vindictiveness, being firm but not angry.

Be patient in all that I permit to happen to you. It is much easier to be meek under circumstances wherein the world praises or pities you than in those wherein the world criticizes or scorns you. True patience extends to all the conditions surrounding the matter which requires patience. If you suffer in your good name, be patient in this loss to yourself, and equally patient in the loss it causes to your loved ones.

To be truly patient in sickness, for example, is to be meek in the particular sickness I permit to befall you with all its pains and sufferings. Do not say, "I could bear this sickness patiently if only it did not prevent my doing my work, or if only it did not last so long; if only this weakness were not part of it, or if only my headache would ease; if only I were somewhere else, or if only it did not cause so much inconvenience for others." No, accept it all, completely, in every one of its circumstances.

This does not mean that you should hide or disregard your illness. Try to get well by doing what is reasonably called for. It is not complaining to tell a doctor your symptoms, quietly and fully, without exaggerating or minimizing; nor is it impatience, but rather in accord with true humility, to apply to yourself the remedies and sedatives he prescribes.

So also with other circumstances that befall you: poverty, overwork, loss, ridicule, failure, the upsetting of your plans. Offer to me all your pains and penalties, uniting them to the pains and penalties I suffered for you. This is the beginning of patience.

Patience with Oneself

> Wait on God with patience.
>
> ECCLESIASTES 2:3

If it is hard to be patient with others and with your circumstances, it is far harder to be truly patient with yourself. Does this seem illogical? Do you think nothing could be easier than to be patient with your own failings? To be truly patient with yourself is extremely difficult. It means being humble enough to accept your limitations, being willing to serve me day after day despite your falls, being content for the time being with your discontents. It means, with Paul, glorying in your weakness. It means recognizing with Philip Neri that the harder you sweep the more dust you raise. It means understanding with Francis of Assisi your own utter nothingness.

Patience with yourself is not thinking too much of your own miseries, but correcting yourself in gentleness, even as you would correct me in your neighbor.

Recognize your faults. More than this, recognize your nothingness; but do not give way to anger at yourself. Be gently firm and firmly gentle, as you resolve with my help to do better in the future.

Should your imperfections momentarily gain the upper hand, you do well to be displeased at your faults; but you do even better to tell me that you are glad to learn your weakness. Since you are full of imperfections, you must expect to be guilty of them over and over. When you allow yourself to become dejected over your involuntary faults, it is because you think you are better than you really are. And once you allow your imperfections to upset you, you are likely to find yourself in a sharp-tongued, irritable mood in all that you do.

When will you learn that of yourself you can do nothing?

It gives me far more glory to correct your faults in my own time than for you to fret about them. Don't you know that I regard your spiritual imperfections in much the same way as I do your physical defects? When you fall sick, not through deliberate neglect, I do not blame you. When you grow tired and hungry I do not look on you with disfavor. When you burn yourself and utter an exclamation of pain, I know: this is natural. So, too, when you are "burned" mentally or emotionally and you exclaim in the form of some imperfection, I know this also is natural. When you give way to involuntary faults in the trials that befall you, I do not hold you to account any more than I do when you become sick or tired or hungry. Accept these unwilled, spontaneous imperfections in exactly the same way that you accept sickness, realizing that the illness is not your fault, but the fault of your nature and your circumstances.

I want your love and your trust. All the rest that is necessary I will do. Let the knowledge of your imperfections lead you to throw yourself on my mercy and love. There is no better way to make progress than this.

Accept yourself for the time being as you are, with all your faults and weaknesses, while resolute in your determination to serve me as best you can. This is a sure sign that self-love is diminishing and spiritual progress is under way.

Accept the truth that I have different plans for all my creatures, and set yourself to carrying out faithfully in every detail my plan for you. This is patience; this is humility; this is holiness.

There is a still higher form of patience, and this, strange as it may seem, is patience with me. So many of my friends try to force me, to push me, to move faster than grace. Not you, my other self, not you!

Patience with me is simply trust in me. To trust me completely is the utmost in patience. To know that I love you more than you love yourself, to realize that I see all your needs and have planned perfectly for their satisfaction, to allow me to shape your life, your progress, your prayers—such is the meekness and patience I desire in you.

Patience with me is loving my will, giving yourself over to me, being indifferent to what I send or permit to befall you, so long as you do not offend me; Patience with me is refusing to be discouraged because of desolations or seemingly slow progress in spirituality.

Patience with me is letting me mold you in my own way, not regarding me as harsh because I send you trials to strengthen you or because I feed your love for me and strip your self-love in ways that cause you pain.

Patience with me is hope in me, seeking your delight in me, trusting your life to me in all its details. Give me this patience, knowing that I love you beyond all tenderness, beyond the power of even my own Mother to know or describe.

Rest in me, my other self, and I will make your goodness shine like the light.

Two Axioms for Patience

> Your patient endurance will be
> your salvation.
>
> LUKE 21:19

If you would exercise patience, strive to do in the emotional and rational order what the sufferer from heart trouble does in the physical order. He moves deliberately, walks slowly, works methodically. He restrains eagerness and excitement, is never violent. If men will do this for physical health, surely you will do it also for spiritual health.

I give you these two axioms for acquiring patience: Do not hurry; do not raise your voice. Hurry produces tension, mistakes, irritation. Raising your voice tends to destroy peace and serenity.

Here is what you shall do.

In the morning make your act of abandonment, giving yourself over to me, and accepting with indifference all that I shall allow to happen to you throughout the coming day. This will do much to tranquilize your mind and soul.

But remember that you are a creature of soul and body and that what the body does affects the soul. You must also hold your body in peace. When you arise, therefore, do so in plenty of time to allow you to dress unhurriedly. Are you coming to Mass? Leave early enough so that you may go serenely. When you eat, do so calmly and deliberately. When you rise from the table to be about your work, again do it in a calm and tranquil manner.

All through the day, preserve this unhurried, calm, leisurely tranquility. Should you lose it, bring yourself back to it quietly, without force or agitation. Walk deliberately, speak gently, move calmly. Do one thing at a time. Try to maintain serenity and deliberateness always, but especially in your routine actions: when you get up or sit down; when you rest and when you eat; when you walk, drive a car, or answer the telephone. Slow your actions. Lower your voice; speak calmly, gently. Carry this attitude into your job and you will find yourself doing not only more, but better work. Your mind will function more logically, your emotions will be better controlled, and your spiritual and physical health much improved.

You will discover it is far simpler to quell the first stirrings of anger when they arise. And remember that it is immeasurably easier to check anger before it can arise than to be "angry and sin not." You will heed the admonition of James in his epistle: "Everyone should be quick to listen, slow to speak, slow to get angry. By anger man does not achieve the holiness that God requires."[8]

And you will heed also the Psalmist: "Refrain from anger and put aside wrath; be not incensed lest you do evil. For evildoers shall be destroyed."[9]

Being thus patient, you will find yourself progressing also in all other virtues. The order in the spiritual life is much like that of the material universe: cause and effect, one detail leading into another, and all depending on and leading to your God, your Maker and Sustainer. The whole of the spiritual life tends to simplicity, toward the simple eagerness to do the task I have set for you.

Say with me now, my other self, this prayer for patience:

> Help me, O Master, to learn and love patience.
> When I am tense with worldly affairs, slow my
> steps, quiet my thoughts. When I am tempted to
> anger by the real or fancied violation of my rights
> remind me quickly that I live my life in partner-
> ship with you. Put into my mind the saving
> thought that, as your other self, I must consult
> you before acting. Help me to be kind, meek, and
> humble in the face of insults, deprivations, and
> all injuries. O divine Master, teach me patience,
> teach me serenity, teach me peace.

chapter seven

P R A Y E R

The Need for Prayer

> You shall pray to me; and I will hear you.
>
> JEREMIAH 29:12

Can you maintain the life of your body without food? Neither can you maintain the life of your soul without prayer.

Prayer is one of the principal means whereby you obtain the divine aid you must have to become completely my other self.

You cannot do even the smallest supernatural act without my grace. Except through grace, you cannot make the first motion toward heaven. And grace cannot be earned, bought, or demanded. It is bestowed upon you as my gift.

Though I give every man the essential graces he needs, I have so ordered it that you obtain additional grace in three principal ways: through the Mass, the sacraments, and prayer. Gaining grace, therefore, depends largely on your seeking it, asking for it. If you stop praying, almost surely you will eventually give up the Mass and the sacraments also. You will lose the life of grace; Prayer is absolutely necessary for you; without it, you will never see your God.

Your progress in the spiritual life will be based on prayer. You cannot expect to know me, to serve me, to trust and love me, unless you pray, unless you think of me, talk with me, look at me, listen to me.

Were not my own actions rooted in prayer? Before I set out on my public life I prayed and fasted in the desert. Before I chose the Twelve, I spent the night praying. Before I went forth to win your redemption, I knelt in the Garden of Gethsemani.

Have you ever read that my Mother preached a crusade, wrought a miracle, or founded a religious order? Yet all grace comes to mankind through her. Mary's prayers of intercession count for more in the divine balance than all the crusades, miracles, and religious orders combined.

Do you not see, my other self, that prayer is not a substitute for action but the basis for it? An apostle without prayer is unthinkable. What such a one might seem to accomplish, he would do not through his own puny efforts but through the prayers of others.

I require action; but I must have action firmly founded on prayer. The more you lead a life of prayer, the more fruitful your work must inevitably become. Prayer and action resemble an iceberg. The one ninth of the Mass visible above the water is action; the eight ninths hidden below are prayer.

Be my apostle, then, first by prayer, second by action. Work earnestly, but pray even more earnestly.

Never let a day pass without prayer, vocal and mental. Speak to me, realizing that I am within your soul and that I see, hear, know, and understand you. Talk to me as to your dearest friend, nay, more, as to your other self.

Never omit your daily prayers, your daily communions with me. Shorten them, if you must, but do not ever omit them.

The more you must do, the more need you will have to work calmly and serenely; and prayer is the key to peace.

My desire is that you should be so perfect that you may enter immediately upon the Beatific Vision when you die. Such perfection is achieved through your wholehearted cooperation with grace, especially the call of grace to prayer, the Mass and the sacraments, and to mortification. You must conquer your passions, root out attachments to creatures, pull up the weeds that choke your growth in me; you must deprive your mind and body of all that leads you away from me. Just as a runner builds up his legs and wind by persistent exercise, so you must practice these deprivations; and just as the runner carries on when his body cries out for rest, so you must persevere. Do so, and eventually you will find your earthly cravings easier to resist and perhaps that they have all but disappeared.

Through prayer, the Mass, and the sacraments particularly this will be accomplished. Through them you will gain the desire and the ability to want only my will. Illogical as it may seem, after you have prayed, even fruitlessly to all appearances, simply uniting your will with mine and striving to be indifferent to all other sentiments, you will find it much easier to want and to do my will.

Just as a child by more perfect obedience, greater love, and fervent petition wins extra favors from his parents, so you win favor with me by your more perfect obedience, greater love, and fervent selfless prayer. Never forget this difference, however: The child does not rely on his parents for the impulse to obey, to love, or to pray; you, on the other hand, depend completely on me for the inspiring graces which, first, give you the desire to please me, and, second, the means actually to do so.

So I say to you, my other self: Pray! Pray! Pray!

How to Pray

> The following, then, must be the pattern of
> your prayer.
>
> MATTHEW 6:9

Do you ask me, as my disciples did, "Lord, teach us to pray"? I will teach you how to pray in all that you think, say, or do. Do not worry about methods. Leave your prayer in my hands. I will give you the way of prayer that is best for you, changing it as you progress, a way that unites your will most firmly with mine.

When you pray, will to give me all of yourself: all of your attention, all of your memory, all of your love. Will to keep nothing back. Whether or not you succeed in giving me all of your attention and memory is not important; the *willing* of it is the core of all true prayer.

Now let me tell you how you may say some of the prayers that are especially dear to my heart. When you pray the Rosary or any other formal prayer, do not race. Pray calmly, meditatively, maintaining yourself in peace and serenity. So many of my friends rush through the Rosary as though it were a foreign language, full of strange words and queer phrases.

There is no such word as "wombJesus," my other self.

When in the "Hail Mary," you say, "pray for us sinners," you ask my Mother to pray not only in your favor but in your stead. You ask her to make your prayer her prayer. Realize that my Mother prays with and for you, making up what your prayer lacks, and unite your prayer with hers.

When you pray the Rosary, unite yourself with its mysteries. Remember that you share in whatever I did as if you had done it yourself. Join yourself to me in my agony; make it your agony. Make my scourging your scourging, my crowning with thorns your crowning, my carrying the cross your carrying the cross, my crucifixion your crucifixion. Join yourself to me in all these mysteries, attaching your sufferings, mortifications, pains, and sorrows to mine, so that our sacrifice may become one sacrifice; one act of love utterly pleasing to the Trinity.

So, too, unite yourself with me in my Resurrection and Ascension. As I gave glory to the Trinity through them, so you also give glory to the Triune God by sharing in them, making them yours as though you had done them yourself.

Unite yourself with the Apostles receiving the Holy Spirit. Join yourself to my Mother in her acceptance of the eternal will and plan. Say with her, "Behold the servant of the Lord; be it done according to your will." Make her fiat your fiat. Unite yourself with her as she visits Elizabeth in charity, and her visit becomes your visit. Unite yourself with Mary in her Assumption and Coronation. As she gave glory to the Trinity through them, so you also give glory to God by sharing in them as though you had experienced them yourself.

Do this not for yourself alone, but for all men. Make atonement for them as I make atonement for you. I wish you to help all men; the living and the souls in purgatory share in your atonement as though they did it themselves.

Do all this in serenity. Pray easily, calmly, not trying to force yourself to "feel" anything, but maintaining a simple peaceful desire to pray the prayer I give you at this and every moment.

Should you be inadvertently distracted, do not fret. Pray more slowly if you wish. A single "Our Father" prayed slowly and with abandonment is far better than many said quickly and carelessly. I do not tally up the number of your prayers.

Concentrate on a word or phrase. Take the "Our Father," for example, and draw all the meaning you can out of the word "Father" or the word "our" or the word "heaven." Or take such a phrase as "Thy will be done," and penetrate to its hidden depths of meaning.

If the distractions persist, simply unite your will with mine in abandonment, submission, and humility and offer your distractions to me. Say that you would rather be distracted, since it appears to be my will for you at that moment, than to enjoy the greatest possible concentration and consolation.

Unite your abandonment to your distracted prayer with my abandonment to the will of my Father, with Mary's fiat, with the abandonment of all the saints, and all holy souls, past, present, and to come.

Unite your submission with my submission in becoming man and in obeying faithfully those whom the Father placed over me in the natural order.

Unite your humility with my humility when I accepted the sentence of death from Pilate; with my humility when I took up the cross and when I fell to the ground to be beaten, kicked, and cursed; with my humility in being driven like an animal through the streets of Jerusalem under the eyes of my own Mother; with my humility in accepting the help of Simon and in making no attempt to hide my tortured face, but gratefully receiving the ministrations of Veronica; with my humility in consoling the holy women; with my humility in being stripped and crucified.

When you pray, whether it be the Rosary, the Way of the Cross, or any other prayer, unite yourself with me as a victim, perfectly abandoned and obedient to the will of my Father, perfectly humble in being the person he wishes you to be, perfect in love.

Ceaseless Prayer

> Always be joyful. Never cease praying.
>
> 1 Thessalonians 5:16–17

As you continue faithfully to pray, your prayer will grow simple, trusting, abandoned.

You will understand more clearly the meaning of my words: "If you ask me for anything in my name, I will do it"[1]

You will know with a deep satisfaction that this is a blank check on the divine treasury. You will make your petitions with a loving confidence that they must surely be answered in the best way and at the best time. You will be persevering in prayer but never willful, stubborn, or nagging. You will remind me, saying "Lord, remember," but you will never nag.

You may say as did my Blessed Mother when she found me in the temple at Jerusalem, "Child, why did you behave toward us in this way? Oh, our hearts were heavy—your father's and mine—as we searched for you!"[2] Here was a mother's gentle question about something she did not understand.

So, too, you may pray when you are mystified, "Lord, my other self, why have you done this?"

My Mother's "prayer" at Cana was a simple statement, "They have no wine."[3] As you became more and more fully my other self, your prayer, too, will take this form, "Lord, they have no wine. Lord, we need you."

And how much more quickly than thought itself will I reply!

Mary and Martha prayed thus, "Please, Master, your dear friend is ill."[4] They knew how I loved Lazarus.

When I came to Bethany after Lazarus was four days in the tomb, they said, "Master, if you had been here, my brother would not have died."[5]

This is the prayer of my other selves: an almost wordless plea, a statement of fact, full of loving trust, humility, and patience, founded on the certain knowledge that I will do what is truly best.

I have promised you, my other self, that I would teach you to pray always. To pray always is simply to direct all that you think, say, or do to me. It is to unite all your thoughts, words, and actions with my will.

How shall you do this?

Begin the day with prayer and offer all of that day to me. Participate with me, if possible, in the Holy

Sacrifice of the Mass and join yourself sacramentally to me in Holy Communion.

Set aside some moments for daily meditation. In our next conversation I will tell you how to meditate.

Pray the Rosary every day if possible. And if you have time and it accords with your state of life, pray part or all of the Divine Office.

Every day do some spiritual reading, especially the Gospels or other parts of Scripture.

Do I ask too much? Think of the time you spend daily in idleness, daydreaming, and useless conversation, in dawdling over the newspaper, in romantic reading and watching television.

Are there not many niches in your day into which prayer would fit perfectly? Can you not pray a decade of the Rosary as you walk along the street, as you drive your car, as you do some household chore? Can you not think of me as you walk up or down stairs, from one room to another, as you move to answer the telephone?

I would have you develop such a free heart that you will go from prayer to work and from work to prayer as though they were one continuous action. Offer your work to me just as you offer your prayer. You do not leave me behind when you go from prayer to the daily duties I have given you. I am with you, I am within you, I am continually giving you energy and inspiration to do your work well.

Only, as you work, do not forget to glance toward me frequently. Do not forget to think quietly, "I do this for you, my other self." Even as you mingle with others, you can still withdraw often to recall my presence within you and to exchange a glance, a thought, or a word with me.

No matter how busy you are, take time out for prayer, even if only for a loving glance. It is the wisest investment of your time you can make. The few seconds it requires to raise your mind to me are richly repaid by deeper peace and keener mental efficiency.

Such recollection will help you guard against overeagerness and hurry. It will prevent your being unduly absorbed in affairs of the moment. It will aid you to remember that I am not so much interested in the quantity of your works as in how well you do each task for me. I ask no more than that you live for me moment by moment, doing your reasonable best in calm serenity.

Thus you will pass your days in union with me, praying always, giving glory always, being my other self in all that you think, say, or do.

Again I say to you: Pray! Pray! Pray!

Do not tell me that you are too busy to lift your thoughts to me.

Give me of your time, and I will do half and more of your work.

Give me your thoughts, and I will enlighten your mind.

Give me your will, and I will return to you my peace.

Give me your love, and I will fill your days with joy.

Give me your prayers, and I will open to you the inexhaustible treasures of heaven.

Meditation

> I will meditate on all thy works.
>
> PSALM 76:13

If you would advance in prayer, my other self, it is necessary for you to meditate. To meditate is simply to think prayerfully about God or the things of God.

Here is a simple way.

Call to your mind that the Trinity dwells in you and that you are in truth my other self. At first it may require a moment or more of deliberate thought to do this. As your prayer becomes simpler, however, this recollection of the presence of your God will come more easily to your mind. Finally it may be habitual. You will need only to lift your mind from your occupation of the moment and your attention will swing to me. I may give you the grace even to be recollected in the midst of your work.

As you begin your meditation, it may be helpful to make brief acts of adoration, sorrow for sin, and petition for my aid.

Having placed yourself in my presence in this way, read prayerfully a passage in the New Testament, go back over one of our conversations, or read whatever of a spiritual nature appeals to you. Read a little, then talk with me about it: What have you read? How does it apply to you? What influence should it have in your life?

You may find later that you meditate better without a book, or that you can do your spiritual reading as preparation for your meditation, not as part of the meditation itself. But rarely will you be able to meditate profitably, in the beginning at least, unless either you use a book or you have made some advance preparation. Otherwise you may waste much time trying to decide what the subject of our conversation should be.

There are many methods that may help you enter into conversation with me. You may reflect on the "Our Father" or the "Apostles' Creed," a word or a phrase at a time, as I told you in our last talk. You may call vividly to mind some scene from my life, causing yourself to see, to hear, to live it. You may place yourself beneath my cross on Calvary, in the upper room at the Last Supper, in Bethlehem, at my birth. You may picture heaven. You may plunge yourself in imagination into hell. You may visualize yourself at the Last Judgment, imagining your joy if you can look to me with confidence, or your despair if you have condemned yourself to eternal doom.

In considering my passion and death do not try to make yourself sad. Forced sentiments have no place in prayer. It is enough if you draw from your reflections and conversation with me good resolutions and a calm, loving knowledge of my love for you.

Your resolutions should be short and specific: I will be kind to this particular person when I meet him today. I will obey cheerfully when I am directed to do this particular task that I dislike. I will smile and say a kind word to this neighbor who gets on my nerves and whom I have been avoiding. I will do some specific task that I have been shirking, and I will do it calmly and conscientiously.

Complete your meditation by asking me to shower my grace upon your soul, to help you grow in humility and in attachment to me, to lead you to complete abandonment, to assist you to be the person I desire, to help you to see me in others, to make you fully and completely my other self.

Lastly, offer a word of thanks for my help and a plea to my Mother to keep you faithful to your resolves.

Meditation will help you to be recollected during the rest of the day. To achieve this recollection, select some outstanding thought that you can frequently call to mind. Choose what most appeals to you:

Abandonment to my Father's will.

Being the person I desire.

The Trinity dwelling in you.

The realization that you are my other self.

The intention of doing all for me and solely for me.

Complete acceptance of the present moment.

Make this concept the dominant note in your day. Use it to fill in the chinks of idleness between your tasks.

If, after weeks or perhaps days, one concept becomes routine, do not be afraid to adopt another. You are not chained; you may freely roam the pastures of prayer. Although I do not want you to flit from method to method, trying now this, now that, with a feverish fretfulness as you search for new thrills and consolations, neither do I want you to remain slavishly bound to one method, fearing to depart from it in any particular, lest I frown on you. Preserve your serenity, an unfettered soul, a free heart.

After a short while you may be able to return to your earlier concept with new recollection.

Another essential for preserving recollection and thus praying always is the habit of ejaculatory prayer. A hundred times and more a day lift up your heart and mind, uniting them to the Father, the Holy Spirit, and me. Gaze on the Trinity dwelling within you. Prostrate yourself in spirit at the foot of the cross. Offer the Father your sacrifices and your joys as a child offers a bouquet of flowers.

If circumstances require it, these little offerings can take the place of many other forms of prayer. Without them, a life of recollection is well-nigh impossible.

If your meditations are not fruitful and consoling, refuse to be discouraged. Do not seek to drive your mind to any particular thoughts. Read a while, then calmly reflect and talk with me; then read again and talk again until your time for meditation is ended. Be patient and persevering; do not fret or worry.

At other times while you are reading and reflecting, you may feel drawn to make acts of love, adoration, thanksgiving, reparation, and petition.

This is as it should be. It is what I desire. Your reading, reflection, and imaginings are only a means; love is the goal. Let your heart make these acts when you feel so inclined. You meditate not merely to learn more, but to love more. Be faithful and I will help your love to grow until it knows almost no limit.

Advanced Mental Prayer

He . . . withdrew to lonely places to pray.
LUKE 5:16

If you persevere, a time will come when meditation will no longer be enough. You will find yourself unable, without great difficulty, to reflect and reason in prayer. This will be almost habitual, not just an occasional state. To reflect will fatigue your mind. To reason will be not only distasteful but almost impossible. You will be carried away by simple thoughts which may inspire you to acts of love and praise. Should you try to turn back to your customary reflections or to ordinary conversation with me about some mystery of my life, you will be discontented, your mind will wander and your will may keep returning to your acts of love.

These are signs that you are ready to advance in prayer.

When this occurs, remember that I have told you what to do. If you cannot reflect and converse as you have customarily done, and if you feel that this is not due to fatigue or indifference, do not force yourself. Abandon your intellect, memory, and will to my hand. Perhaps you can let simple acts of love, trust, thanksgiving, and praise fill your meditation period. At other times acts may have no meaning and you may use them simply to lull the imagination and curb distractions.

Again, instead of making a variety of acts, you may feel inclined to repeat one and the same aspiration over and over: "My God, I love you." "My God and my All." "Thy will be done."

Still later, the number of repetitions of this aspiration may dwindle. You will no longer want to talk, but rather just to look at your God, to rest in me, not making any act so much as merely breathing it or living it.

Simplicity will not be achieved overnight. How fast it grows will depend on how wholeheartedly you abandon yourself to me. Sometimes you will easily be able to meditate in the old way, other times not at all. When you can meditate without driving and fatiguing yourself, do so. When you cannot, let your prayer consist of simple acts or of resting in me.

Outside of prayer, you will be able to reflect, reason, and consider just as well as ever, but not while you are *in* prayer. Once your prayer has advanced beyond meditation you will be able to talk about spiritual matters and to study the truths of the faith in much the same way as you talk and study mathematics and science, but outside of, not in, prayer. When you pray you will no longer be able to meditate; and when you meditate it will no longer seem like prayer, but rather like study.

You are being readied for forms of prayer in which your soul will have no other attitude than that of waiting in a kind of passivity, a profound quiet, making no effort to reason, to imagine, to understand, but gently loving your God with a peaceful will.

You are being readied for contemplative prayer.

Contemplative prayer, my other self, is not necessary for sanctity. Some of my great saints were never contemplatives. But neither is contemplative prayer reserved for those in the religious state. I bestow this special gift more readily upon the religious because they give me more fully of their understanding, memory, and imagination. But I desire to give contemplative prayer also to those in the lay and active life, if only they will stop throwing obstacles in my way.

Silence is one of the predispositions for contemplation, not merely exterior silence, but the interior quiet that proceeds from detachment from passion and prideful desires. The silent soul is dead to the shrill cries of selfishness.

Though such silence is easier to attain in the cloister, it is also achieved by many in the active life who sincerely and prayerfully seek it.

If you would advance in prayer, therefore, refrain from too much idle conversation, light reading, daydreaming, from too many worldly amusements, from too much concern about finances, security, and worldly affairs. Withdraw now and then into solitude.

This does not mean that you should live an abnormal life. If your duty requires activity in worldly affairs, do what accords with that duty. You should not make yourself an eccentric by withdrawing from reasonable and necessary social contact.

No matter how active your exterior life may be, you can maintain interior "silence" by following the instructions and using the help I give you.

I have told you how you must strive to do one thing at a time and each thing for me, not for human respect or profit; how you must try to do the task of the moment perfectly; how you must work calmly and without worry; how you must use ejaculatory prayers, turning your mind to me in fleeting glances many, many times a day; how you must fill in the niches of your day with prayer; how you must set aside regular periods for prayer and spiritual reading. In these periods seek a place where you can be alone with me. Seek the solitude of the Blessed Sacrament or of your own room, the countryside, or the dark.

Do you not see that the principles governing your growth in prayer are the same as those that govern all that pertain to the spiritual life? First, the ardent desire to do my will. Second, the firm trust that I watch over you, protect you, guide you, live within you. Third, the giving of yourself to me without reserve, holding nothing back.

That is why I repeat so often that you must seek, desire, will only the prayer I give you at any particular moment. Whatever prayer I will for you should be the prayer you will for yourself.

Trust me, though your prayer should seem totally empty, a waste of time, even disgusting to you.

Give me your entire being in prayer: all of your thoughts, all of your memories, all of your imaginings, and, most important, all of your will.

Come to pray humbly, recognizing that of yourself you cannot pray at all.

Come generously, offering all your faculties and powers of soul and body.

Come trustfully, realizing that whatever I do is perfect.

Come lovingly, telling me that you want my will and that alone.

Pray thus and your prayer of that moment is perfect. No saint can pray better.

Arid Prayer

> My heart within me is desolate.
>
> PSALM 142:4

There is a certain similarity, my other self, between the growth of married love and the growth of love for me. When lovers marry, they are filled with an urgent desire to be together. They want to shut out the rest of the world while they repeat over and over their sentiments of affection. It seems, then, that no sacrifice could be too difficult to be attempted. Each would give up everything for the other in a wild, impulsive gesture.

But this love is largely the self-gratification of being in love with love. Having met the tests of a good and successful marriage, another love emerges, one that is far deeper and truer. Seeking more the happiness of the spouse and less concerned with personal gratification, it expresses itself daily in a thousand practical, sacrificial ways. Whereas before the lover may have assured his beloved that he would make any sacrifice for her (and in assuring her have also been assuring himself), now he knows he would truly do what before he merely protested perhaps that he would do.

Your love for me develops somewhat similarly. When I bestow special graces and consolations to call you more closely to my side, you may be almost surfeited with joy and with a passion to serve me. Nothing seems too difficult for you to attempt: no penance, no fasting, no regimen of prayer.

But there comes a time for testing your love. Gradually I withdraw my consolations. No matter what you do, aridity and dryness, unfruitfulness and sterility in prayer become more frequent. Do you love me or my consolations? Will you continue to pray when the pleasures of prayer are withdrawn?

In this aridity you want to pray as of old, but you lack the joy and peace of old. You want to give me your attention, but you cannot. You feel, therefore, that you are not praying, that you accomplish nothing, that you are wasting time. So you begin to want to do something else: to make "forced acts" of prayer, and when these also fail to bear sensible fruit, you want to turn to reading, studying, or talking with someone. You may even experience a deep distaste for the thought of prayer.

You must not allow this dryness to turn you back to meditative and less simple prayer. Though you find it easier to read than simply to "wait," if in your reading you see that you are not "praying," then do not read. Though you may find it possible to think about my humanity and passion, unless you are able to think of them prayerfully—not as you do when you are simply organizing your thoughts, studying, or arranging a talk—do not do it. Stay in your prayer of arid waiting. Offer it to me, tell me that you want it since I send it to you, and that you desire nothing else.

I am testing you, my other self. I must see whether you pray because it is my will, or because praying makes you feel "good," "devout," and "at peace."

When I test you thus, how wearying, dry, and tasteless your prayer becomes! How your soul plods along, footsore and weary, hungering for me, sometimes seeming ready to die of thirst for me!

You want to contemplate truth; you want to sing my praises, offer thanks, express your love. And because you want so much to love me, seeing how much I love you, the pain in your soul is like that of an open wound. Trust me. Not to sing is better for you at this moment than to sing. I am shaping your prayer. Trust me.

This is the critical time. Persevere. In those moments when you have nothing to give me but your dry will, and when you offer it with all your painful generosity, then you are immeasurably dear to me. Then indeed I am helping you, watching anxiously, full of compassion for your pain, waiting to reward you, quick to ease your suffering the moment it appears to be too keen.

This is when you need to be patient in prayer, to rest content with whatever I give you. If you cannot think, do not try to think. If you cannot talk, do not try to talk. You can always rest; and the prayer of rest at that moment is exactly what I want of you.

You will be tempted to pry into your prayer, to see how and what you are doing. Resist this temptation. Renounce yourself. Renounce your understanding and memory. Give them over to me to do with as I wish. Accept the prayer I give you. Want nothing else. Tell me that you desire no thoughts, no memories, except those I choose to bestow.

Should you see yourself distracted and curious to know how you are praying, simply return your attention gently and calmly to my presence within you.

How well Francis knew my mind when he said: "Stay in your prayer, and when distractions attack you, turn them away gently, if you can; if not, put the best face you can on it and let the flies bother you as much as they like whilst you are talking to your God. He does not mind that. You can brush them away with a gentle, calm movement but not with an alarm or impatience that would upset you."[6]

And again: "One may continue in God's presence not only by hearing him, seeing him, or speaking to him, but also by waiting to see if it may please him to look at us, to speak to us, or to make us speak to him: or yet again, by doing nothing of all this, but by simply staying where it pleases him for us to be, and because it pleases him for us to be there."[7]

Among the greatest mortifications you can offer me is the loss of the sensible joy of the presence of your God once you have experienced it. Yet this is but the shadow of the mortification I myself offered in Gethsemani. There the incomprehensible joy of the

Beatific Vision did not prevent spiritual sorrow in my soul or agony in my human nature.

My other self, you can emulate me faintly by offering to your God the desolation you experience in aridity. You can even offer the willingness never again to have the joys of my consoling presence in this life, if such be my will for you.

A Foretaste of Heaven

> That your love may become richer and richer. . . .
>   PHILIPPIANS 1:9

In prayer I sometimes do to you as I did to my Apostles when they were fishing in Galilee after my Resurrection. Peter and the others had fished all night, taking nothing. When day broke, they saw me standing on the shore; but they did not know me. I asked them if they had caught anything, and when they said, "No," I told them, "Cast your net to the right of the boat."[8]

They did, and the catch was enormous—153 large fish.

So I do to you in prayer. You try to pray for a long time and "take nothing." You are desolate. Grievances, distractions, irritations surround you on every side. But over and over you keep offering this suffering to me, telling me you do not want to change it or stop it, asking me only to help you endure it. Then, when you are tired and perhaps distressed, I say to you, "Stay a little longer. Cast your net again." And suddenly you also have a great catch.

It may happen before the Blessed Sacrament or at Mass, in your room, or anywhere. Suddenly you *know* and you say: "You are Christ, the Son of the living God, and you are also my Brother. I cannot see you or feel your presence, but I do not ask for that. I am content to live by faith alone."

With a certain knowledge more sure than if you could see me, you may know that I am within you, that I have made my abode with you, that I live within you.

You become like Mary of Bethany listening at my feet, tranquil, silent, peaceful, in repose; or like John reclining on my breast at the Last Supper. So deep will this peaceful repose be at times that your soul will seem in a sense to sleep in the delight and satisfaction of the presence of your God.

My other self, should I call you to this state of prayer, stay still. Make no acts. Say no words. Seek no thoughts.

During this sleep of the soul your intellect may be flooded with light and inspiration, so that you see truths that you have never really perceived before. It may be a vivid realization of the beauty of your God, so clear that for the moment you understand with a deep knowledge and conviction that beside him all things, all glories, are as nothing.

It may be the realization that your God truly holds you, as it were, in the palm of his hand, so that you can do literally nothing without him.

It may be a new knowledge that you should love me not only as God but also as man.

It may be a sudden realization of how eager I am to grant your requests. You know while you are in this prayer that anything you ask of me will surely be given to you. In a calm, peaceful way, without in any way disturbing your repose, you may perhaps begin to shower me with unspoken petitions: that no soul should be lost this day; that sinners should be converted; unbelievers enlightened; the souls in purgatory released; your family especially blessed; sufferers strengthened.

And should you find yourself hurrying, trying to get all of your petitions "in" before this moment of special favor should pass, in the next instant you may know that I am smiling very tenderly upon you and that I am saying to you, "Don't hurry. I shall not leave you. I live in you. I shall always hear your prayers just as I do now."

Then, touched by a special grace, you may perhaps ask me, again without words, that you might always love me with your whole self and that, with the Little Flower, you might be the victim of my merciful love, that the love which inflames my Heart and which is pent up there might be pierced by the arrow of your willingness to suffer for me, and that a current of love might connect my divine Heart with your poor heart. Above all, you may ask that in everything you say, do, or think, you should do my will. All this you will do, or know, intuitively. It will require no words, no thought, no effort. I will "touch" you, and your knowledge and love will suddenly be immeasurably multiplied.

Yes, my other self, mystical graces may transform your life, little by little, then faster and faster, until finally I lift you to the glorious pinnacle of transforming union. It will not be done in a moment, and it cannot be done by you. In contemplation I do all or nearly all. You do almost nothing but give me your will. There may be raptures in which your soul neither sees nor knows anything but me.

How surely you advance when you accept, and will, only the prayer I give you!

Should I confer on you this priceless gift of contemplative prayer, do not, I beg you, allow yourself to become puffed up. Remember that he to whom I give much will be expected to return much. Be grateful, but do not allow yourself to become attached to this or any other divine favor. At all times, be ready equally to possess or to give up spiritual and material favors, with the single exception of my life-giving grace.

Do you not see how precious it would be if I should lead you into this prayer? In its fullness this state may even be carried over into your daily routine, so that while you are attentive to your duties, in the depths of your soul you are also habitually recollected and attentive to your God. You will know as you work that you are doing my will, and you will refer it all to me in the consciousness that I am living within you.

Do you not see in this, my other self, a certain similarity, though infinitely removed from it, to my own perpetual contemplation of the Beatific Vision in my earthly life in Palestine? I contemplated the Trinity face to face at all times, even as I carried on my ordinary duties. Conscious of hunger, pain, joy, sorrow, the needs of others, teaching and listening, yet my human soul at every moment beheld the Trinity face to face.

Think of this, my other self, and know that if you persevere faithfully in prayer and meditation, I may give you in my own good time this immense blessing of advanced mystical prayer, even the prayer of union, a sign of the Beatific Vision that I have planned to be yours for all eternity.

chapter eight

AVOIDANCE OF SIN

What Sin Is

> You . . . rejoice in a thing of naught.
>
> AMOS 6:14

Do you know what sin is, my other self?

It is evil and the source of evil. It is the misuse of life. Mortal sin is the expulsion of God from your soul.

I have come to dwell within you. To put you at ease I hide my majesty, donning a disguise so lowly that you often forget my greatness completely and frequently do not even know I am present. I give you the most precious riches, access to an endless deposit of grace, and I do it so quietly that you do not even know what you are receiving. Dwelling within you, I help you throughout your life on earth to prepare for eternal glory.

At all times I am ready to talk with you. When you are in need, I am always present, smoothing your path, warding off evil. When I permit evil to touch you, I give you all the help you need to combat it, and more. I require not even a word to make me spring to your side; a glance, a mere trace of a thought, is enough.

All I ask is that you accept me as your King, not to be feared cravenly, but to be loved.

The house of your soul is a clay hut, dark, uncomfortable, infirm, threatening always to fall to pieces. Nevertheless, I will live there. I will repair this house of your soul. I will brighten it, furnish it, make it glorious. All I ask is your willing acknowledgment that I am your King. Such acknowledgment is holiness. To refuse to acknowledge me as King is sin.

Sin then is a turning away from your King toward some creature, living or inanimate. I will not reveal myself, here in your house, in all my glory. If I did, you could not turn away. But creatures are permitted to reveal themselves in alluring, enticing splendor.

When you gaze at created goods and are tempted to deny me by putting them before me, I call to you through conscience: "Look at me. Fasten your eyes on me and do not turn away."

If the matter is not of grave consequence and you say, "You are my King and I acknowledge it, but I want this forbidden creature, too," that is a venial sin. You hurt me and set up obstacles to my love for you, but you do not force me to leave you.

But if you say: "You are no longer my King. I choose to be the slave of this creature," then I must depart. I will not dwell where I am not welcome. And your house instantly becomes fearfully dark and the devil comes to make it his home.

This is sin: Ordering your God out of your soul.

It is the utmost tragedy.

All the evils in the world come from the abuse of free will. Nothing that I have made is evil of itself. I cannot create evil; I permit it only that good may come of it. By refusing free will to angels and men, I could have prevented evil from entering the universe. But the gift of free will to persons who can obey or disobey is a greater good than a world filled with creatures devoid of freedom.

It is from the sins of angels and of men that all uncleanness comes. Adultery, murder, theft, malice, deceit: these make a man unclean. A proud man is unclean. A blasphemous man is unclean. An envious man is unclean. They have taken their will away from the service of their God. Cleanness is not only akin to Godliness, it *is* Godliness; for he that is clean has united his will with mine. Untouched by worldly desires, he is pure in his longing that my will be done. Therefore, blessed are the clean of heart, for they shall see God.

Sin brought pain and death into the world. Sin is the breeding ground of poverty and insecurity. It is the seed of suffering, murder, war.

Now do you appreciate more clearly what sin is? Do you see that it is vandalism, like the defacing of a masterpiece of art, like the wanton destruction of a rare painting, a unique statue, a magnificent building? Sin introduces deadly insects and plant diseases into a glorious garden. It sows cockle among the wheat, spoiling the harvest. It attempts to blot out with the acid of disobedience the Divine Architect's blueprint for happiness.

Never think of sin as attractive. Sin is agony; sin is death; sin is the cause of hell.

The Source of All Evil

He who commits sin springs from the devil. . . .
1 JOHN 3:8

Although all evil is the result of sin, nothing that happens, good or evil, occurs without my permission. Good takes place with my smile, evil with my sufferance.

Evil is not unlimited. The devils clamor to do many things with malevolent eagerness, but I restrain them. As Satan desired to have Simon that he might sift him like wheat, so he desires to have you. But I have forbidden him any power over your will.

So sacred is the freedom of your will, my other self, that even I will not overpower it. I urge, aid, and influence you by the impulses I give you, the example I show you, the people with whom I bring you in contact. The final decision, however, to do good or evil must always be made by you. Yours is the choice either to obey or to disobey.

The evil that was done me on Calvary occurred with my Father's permission. He would not obstruct the freedom of men even to commit deicide.

Do you think of the cross as a retribution my Father demanded in atonement for sin? No, it would have been more than enough for me merely to have been born. It was not required that I die. Only, in the eternal wisdom of my Father, it was best that I should give this utmost proof of my love.

How amazing is this freedom of the human will!

As man, I was free to refuse the cross. Prostrate in the garden, I did not have to accept the chalice. My Mother was free to choose or refuse to be my parent. My Father sent his angel with an offer of marriage, and Mary accepted.

My enemies were free to sin or not to sin. They did not have to crucify me.

Does not all this give you a new conception of the great gift of freedom and the horror of sin? Men degraded by sin condemned me; a man weakened by sin permitted me to die; debased by sin, men scourged me, crowned my head with thorns, crucified me.

My passion and death demonstrate what the world would be if the devil held sway. What possessed these Romans that they indulged in such abysmal cruelty? What possessed Pilate to make him so spineless in the face of all that was good in his nature urging him to release me?

What possessed Peter to deny me?

What possessed my disciples to flee in terror through the night?

What possessed Judas to sell me for a small bag of silver?

This is what sin does to men, making them cowards, even fiends. This is how sin wrecks my Father's plan for human happiness.

Do you think of pain, death, hell, as something your God has devised to show his supreme authority, as a parent demonstrates authority in spanking a disobedient child?

Far from being mere punishments in such a sense, they are the effects of sin, the necessary results of sin in the omniscience of your God.

Just as fire burns you when you plunge your hand into the flames, so sin necessarily brings pain and suffering. Because only what is pure can be united with the Trinity in eternal glory, purgatory and hell become necessary for the impure: purgatory to cleanse the soul so that it can be united with God; hell for those who freely choose to have none of me.

In a sense, the sin of Adam and Eve made pain and death necessary. According to the divine plan, in the Father's wisdom, these were the results of their fall.

Just as their sin brought pain and death into the world, so your sins call down pain and suffering not only upon yourself but upon all men. Every sin sows misery not only for the sinner but for his fellow men. Every sin makes the world a less happy place.

If men do not go to heaven alone, neither do they go to hell alone.

Just as it hurts the whole human body when a part of it is injured, so it hurts the whole Mystical Body, my Body, when one of its members sins.

As it gives pleasure to the whole human body when all its members are healthy and sound, so it is with my Mystical Body when its members do well and are honored by the Father.

The fate of the world, my other self, depends in part on you. The eternal welfare of many souls rests somewhat in your hands. It is within your power, through the freedom of your will, to cause the world to be a far worse or a far better place. Your life can help make it, for many, the anteroom of heaven or the vestibule to hell.

Gethsemani

> Then they spat in his face and dealt him
> blows. . . .
>
> MATTHEW 26:67

If you would know what sin is, my other self, study Good Friday and the night before. So terrifying were those hours that my chosen Apostles scattered like frightened birds, and only one of them could bear to watch me die. Listen to him. He will tell you what he saw.

∽❧∾

I am John, the disciple whom Jesus loved.

There are no words, my fellow member of Christ's Body, to tell you how divine our dear Lord is in his love and unswerving purpose or how human in his sorrow and dismay.

He spends the earlier hours of Thursday night giving us, his friends, the gift of his Body and Blood. He talks to us at length, painstakingly telling us that he is going to his Father and that we must not let ourselves be afraid. He warns us that the world will hurl hatred and persecution against us, but he consoles us by promising to send the Holy Spirit and by giving us his own peace and joy.

He prays to the Father for us, that we should all be one. Calling us his friends, he gives us his new commandment of love. He will live on in us, he says, if we but live in him by keeping his commandments. "I am the vine, you are the branches."[1]

He tells us that whatever we shall ask the Father in his name, or whatever we shall ask him in his own name, will be granted.

All this he does with extreme care, repeating himself over and over in different words, explaining to Peter, Thomas, and Philip, who ask him questions, just what he means. Reluctant to leave us, he prolongs the hour of parting, coming back again and again for another word, seeming to ask us, "Do you understand? Are you sure now that you understand?"

And then we go out to the garden and he is overcome by sadness. He tells the eight to sit down while he goes on farther to pray. He takes Peter, James, and me aside. "I am plunged in sorrow, enough to break my heart!" he tells us. "Stay here and keep awake."[2]

Why does he take us three, asking us to watch with him? Is it because he looks to us for pity and comfort? If so, how we failed him!

Going a little way off, but still within our sight, he falls to his knees, and then upon his face, praying.

"Father, you can do all things! Spare me this cup! No, not what I will, but what you will!"[3] Thus he prays for some time.

Rising after a while and coming back to us, he finds us sleeping. We did not want to sleep. We tried to watch with him, but a deep sadness and foreboding overcame us with such fatigue that we could not resist.

He speaks to Peter in his gentle way. "Simon, are you sleeping? Were you not able to stay awake one hour? Keep awake and pray, all of you, that you may not succumb to temptation." And then he adds these words to show how well he knows our human frailty, "The spirit is willing, but the flesh is weak."[4] And that is true. We slept not because we wanted to, but because we were so frail.

Again he goes back to pray, falling on his face. "My Father, if this cup cannot be spared me, and I must drink it, may your will be done."[5]

And after a while he returns a second time; we awaken to find him gazing upon us, and we know not what to say. Without a word of complaint, he resumes his prayer.

An angel from heaven comes to give him strength, for now he falls into an agony. As he prays even more ardently, his sweat falls to the ground as thick drops of blood. And this we see in the full light of the spring moon.

Why does he keep coming back to us between his prayers? It is partly because the sins of the world have laid a crushing burden upon his great Heart, he looks for one to pity and comfort him. But there is no one; and hence he goes back again, alone, to wrestle with dread.

He comes back because, even in his own bitter distress, he is keenly aware of our coming temptation, our need for strength. Peter will soon deny him, yet he urges him to pray. What a lesson this is for us to cling to in our future years. Knowing that Peter will fall, but that Peter does not have to fall, knowing that Peter can find courage through prayer, yet all the time aware that Peter will sleep instead, he urges him to pray.

How sublime that he can think of us, even in his own agony!

How touching that he makes excuse for us: "The spirit is willing, but the flesh is weak."[6]

How human he was in his sorrow; how divine in his love.

The Betrayal

> One in your group will betray me.
>
> JOHN 13:21

After his ordeal in the garden, having won the victory, calm, serene, but terribly grave, He wipes the bloody sweat from his face, rouses us, and goes out to meet his enemies.

Judas is at hand. He brings with him soldiers, servants, and hangers-on, some carrying swords, others clubs, still others lanterns. They want to be very sure to take him this time. They have no need to be anxious. He is willing, he is ready.

Judas breaks away from the crowd. Jesus is standing in front of us. Indeed, it is only his presence that keeps us from running away.

As Judas looks at him, his face so pale, haggard, deep-lined with struggle, what does he think?

Perhaps he thinks: "I cannot do this. I cannot betray my intimate Friend, my Companion, my Teacher." Or perhaps: "I must go through with it. I have taken their money. They're watching me. They will kill me if I play them false. And they have him anyway."

Judas is a coward. He kisses Jesus; as you would go to someone and hold out your hand in a gesture of friendship, he kisses him.

And Jesus says to him, "So this is the errand, my friend, on which you have come!"[7]

Judas knows what he means—why are you doing this?

"Judas, with a kiss you betray the Son of Man?"[8] Is this your friendship, you who were my comrade?

Do you not see how he is showering grace upon Judas' soul, how he seeks to strengthen and save him? Now is the time for Judas to turn on the multitude, flinging the silver in their faces and taking his stand by the side of his Master. It may be too late to save Christ, but not too late to save Judas. But Judas is a coward.

When he has kissed that face, when he hears the soft vibrant voice call him "friend," what thoughts race through his mind? Does his heart almost stop beating as the first despairing pangs of remorse stab him?

At that moment Jesus steps farther forward. "Who is it you are looking for?"

"Jesus," they say, "Jesus of Nazareth."

"I am he!" And there is a force in his manner that causes them all to shrink back, so that those in front fall against those behind and, tripping over one another, they tumble to the ground.

Once more he asks them, and when they reply he says: "I told you that I am he. Therefore, since you are looking for me, let these men go unmolested."[9]

Then Peter draws the sword he carries and strikes at the nearest foe.

It is easy to think about this as though it were only a scene from a play. But it is far different. Peter strikes hard, strikes to kill. His blow is aimed at Malchus, the servant of the high priest, and Malchus, dodging and taking the sword on the side of his head, has his right ear sliced off.

Malchus cries out, the guards start forward. Peter, knife upraised, stands his ground.

But Jesus stops further bloodshed. He makes Peter put away his sword. He approaches Malchus, touches his ear, and instantly it is fully healed.

With this dramatic sign he again gives Judas opportunity to turn back, and not only Judas but all his enemies.

Some of them, indeed, hesitate until goaded by Satan, their leaders seize him.

Encouraged by his resignation, they tie him securely.

And we, his disciples, do nothing. Most of us run away.

The Scourging

> He was bruised for our sins.
>

He does not want us to fight to save him, for he has told Peter to put away his sword.

Nevertheless, we might at least have gone with him, proving to him that our loyalty was greater than our fear. The spirit is willing, but the flesh is weak.

They lead him away.

Gathering the remnants of our courage, Peter and I follow the crowd at a safe distance to the palace of Annas and Caiphas. Since my family and I are known to Annas and his household, they allow me to enter the courtyard while Peter at first stays outside.

Annas questions the Lord about his teachings and his followers. When Jesus says to him: "I have spoken openly. . . . Question those who heard what I said,"[10] a servant strikes him in the face.

This is but one of many blows during that frightful night. Struck often, his face spat upon, blindfolded, and slapped, and called upon to prophesy who has hit him, he is silent. These are heavy blows that jolt his head from side to side. How his head must ache. How nausea must be sweeping over him.

All through the night they torment him. In the morning, after they have condemned him, they lead him to Pilate. You know how Pilate tries to set him free. Sending him first to Herod, he then seeks to release him in accordance with the custom of the Passover, but the multitude chooses Barabbas, the robber and murderer, instead. Pilate has him scourged, hoping that this will satisfy the crowd.

You do not know what a Roman scourging is like. They bind him, naked, to a column in such a way that he can hardly move, and so that every blow may leap upon him with full force.

And they beat him. They beat him with whips that are thongs of hardened leather in which pieces of lead and bone are embedded, with sharp points to tear the flesh.

The blows fall, regularly as a metronome—one—two—three—four—five. The first lashes raise long red welts. Others break the skin and the blood begins to run. Soon flesh hangs down in shreds. Pieces of skin and flesh fly from the bloody back.

With each blow the thongs wrap themselves around the body, the pieces of lead and bone cutting deep and yet deeper. Though the poor body trembles and sags, the thwack! thwack! thwack! thwack! of the scourges continues relentlessly.

Jesus says not a word.

The executioners set their teeth. They will force him to scream. He must beg, he must plead, he must curse; he must not be silent.

Now the blood flows from a hundred wounds and more. It spatters the executioners, the lookers-on, the column, the earth; it collects in a spreading pool at the victim's feet.

Only when Jesus can hardly hold himself on his feet, when dizziness and nausea and weakness cause him to sag helplessly against the column, upheld only by his bound wrists, only then do they stop. They must not kill him. Pilate has not sentenced him to death.

But they are not yet finished; This man, remember, has said he is a king. The body has been torn with scourges, now let us see how the spirit can be racked with ridicule.

They drape a scarlet rag around his shoulder, set him up against the column, place a reed for a scepter in his right hand. Now for a crown!

One of them weaves some thorny plants, kept for firewood in the courtyard, into a kind of crown. The thorns are needle sharp, long, and tough. Setting this crown upon his head, they press and beat it firmly down. Curved thorns cut through the top of the scalp and protrude again at the forehead.

Now a satanic ridicule begins. One by one, the soldiers, who have been called to join in the fun, come before the Lord, bowing and kneeling in mock homage. Snatching the scepter, they beat him on the head, across the face. Blood runs anew over his forehead, around his brows, down his cheeks, along his nostrils; and from his nose blood flows into his beard.

Finally, tired of the game, they return him to Pilate; and even hardened Pilate is startled. "Now look!" he says. "Here is the man!"[11]

Man, indeed! Is this a man, this creature, this worm?

Yes, this is a man and the Victim of men. And this is God.

And this is SIN!

Do you ask, how could men do such fiendish things?

You also could do them. Yes, all of us while on earth could do them.

Given over to sin, we could do all these horrors that now make us cringe and shrivel up inside just to think of them.

This is what sin does to men. This is what sin makes of men, little by little, until the work of destruction is complete, until of their own free will they choose hell.

∽◎∽

The Carrying of the Cross

> He gave them the greatest proof of his love.
>
> JOHN 13:1

Did John's words shock you, my other self, into a new dawning realization of the tragedy of sin?

Can you bear to be shocked still more? Can you endure seeing me carry my cross, hanging upon it, through the eyes of my Mother?

How her heart was torn! Think how your heart would break if you saw your son or your daughter, your husband or wife, your father or mother suffering what I suffered.

How your soul would cry out in sorrow for the bloody, broken body; how it would twist in agony to see the brutal falls to the rough stones; how it would cringe to gaze on the tortured face; how it would scream at the ring of the hammer on the spikes; how your tormented spirit would strive to tear itself from your body at sight of the poor corpus on the gibbet!

Could you bear this anguish?

Had Mary been less than the immaculate one with integrity preserved, could she have witnessed my Passion and not have gone mad?

Listen to Mary, my Mother and your Mother. Listen, if you dare to know more fully what sin is.

~⊙~

My child, among the grievous pains my Son endured was the sight of my own sorrow. I saw him die. In spirit I died with him. I watched his martyrdom; he watched mine. My soul was sorrowful beyond the power of your mind to conceive. His soul was more sorrowful still.

When they led him away to be crucified, they tore off him the red rag they had put on him in ridicule so that once again his wounds opened and the blood began to run anew.

They put on him his own clothing, the seamless garment I had made for him. Immediately it is stained with blood. His garment becomes soggy, for his flesh lies open in so many places.

Bringing him the heavy beam, they lay it on his bruised and beaten shoulder. He staggers under the weight, then starts to walk with weak, uncertain steps after the soldiers.

Golgotha is not far, only an eternity. The street is rough and stony. The jarring of the beam on his shoulder starts the blood flowing afresh from his thorn-covered head. Blinded by blood, he can hardly see where to put his feet. He steps on the side of a stone, loses his balance, and falls.

The wood comes down heavily upon his shoulder and the back of his neck, driving the thorny crown deeper into the head that I had cradled so often against my breast. His fine hair is soggy and matted with bloody mud; his hair that I combed and brushed so tenderly when he was my child.

The soldiers help drag him to his feet. The Lamb goes forward again to the slaughter.

His knees and legs are torn, blood-red and open, those strong, graceful limbs that flashed in the sunlight as he ran gaily in his boy games long ago.

With every step the beam shifts a little on the bruised shoulder. The raw wound widens, the furrow lengthens. Have you ever tried to carry a heavy plank on an uneven path, even one that does not rest on an open wound?

He falls again and again from sheer weakness. Each time the wood crushes him more cruelly to the street. Do you see how, once, the end of the beam smashes with sickening force on the back of his outflung hand? This is the hand that caressed my face, the baby hand I used to kiss, the boy's hand that held wood for Joseph, the physician's hand that healed the sick and disabled, the priest's hand that blessed his people.

Now, utterly drained of strength, he can bear the burden no further. Surely he will die, the soldiers think, unless he is helped. How little they know! He will die when the sacrifice is complete. He will die when he is ready. He alone can offer up his life, he alone can lay it down; no one can take it from him.

Nevertheless, the soldiers do find one to help him: Simon. And I know that he accepts Simon's aid gratefully and richly blesses him for it. And I bless Simon, too. It is right that he who in his earthly life helped so many should not be without help in his last hours.

Now we have reached Golgotha. I told you it was not far. Jesus, my Son, has brought his cross to the scene of execution. The sacrifice, the ransom, the Mass, is about to be offered. My Son will die, so that my sons and daughters may live.

The Crucifixion

Father, forgive them. . . .

LUKE 23:34

Your Lord stands on trembling legs, waiting. . . .

His head is bowed. His strength is gone. Only the will remains indomitable.

They take the beam from Simon and lay it on the ground.

The final act has begun.

They tear his garments from his body. His clothing is glued to his back, his shoulders, his thighs and legs, his arms, even his chest. It has become embedded in the raw wounds and dried blood.

When they rip off his garments, every sore is opened anew. Pieces of flesh are torn from his body. Doctors have written about the agony he must have suffered, about the violent shudder that racked his body, wondering that he did not faint from shock and pain.

What they imagine, I see with my eyes.

His executioners lay him on the cross, stretch out his arms, and mark the spots for the nails.

They seize his hand, holding it firm. The spike is touched to his wrist. The raised hammer falls and the nail penetrates his flesh. They drive it fast.

Yes, my child, doctors writing of this have told you how his thumb with a spasmodic movement strikes against the palm of his hand. They know what this means: the great nerve center in the wrist has been touched. An indescribable flame of pain has shot up through his arm, bursting like a fire bomb in his brain. They have told you that the nerve is not completely cut, only ripped, so that the raw nerve itself remains pressed against the spike, leaving this unbearable agony to be repeated over and over with every movement, no matter how slight; and this goes on for hours.

Doctors have written about what they saw in imagination. You could not bear it if I told you what my eyes beheld.

But this I will tell you. Horrible as is this physical torment, it is not the worst of my Son's agony. Mental agony is worse, mental agony that, later on, will bring from his lips, the psalm of desolation: "My God, my God, why do you abandon me!"[12]

They stretch out his other arm, place the nail, poise the hammer. I saw his face contorted with inexpressible pain a moment ago. I cannot bear to watch it again.

But I cannot help hearing the *sounds* of torture. . . .

They have stopped the hammering. They are lifting him to his feet, raising the beam to which his arms are nailed.

I know nothing of nerve centers. But agony, that I know! Undiluted pain! Convulsive torment!

They move him back against the upright stake which they have fastened securely in the ground. They help him "climb" the stake until, with a sudden effort, they are able to place the beam on top of the upright.

If you could see how his body sags, how it pulls on the poor pierced wrists, how his head drops forward!

Bending his knees so that his feet are flat against the upright, they nail him fast.

Must I go on to the end? Have you not seen and heard enough?

Must I tell you how, for hours, he hangs between heaven, and earth, bereft of respect, of belief, almost friendless, so terribly alone?

Do you see the huge spikes through his wrists and feet? Do you note the torn knees, the countless lacerations, the great welt on his shoulder, the crown of thorns running into and through his scalp, the puffed lips, the swollen nose? Do you see how the flies settle in his sores? How slowly he turns his poor tired head from side to side, like a great heaviness that he can move only by inches and with a mighty effort.

He prays: "Father forgive them. . . ."[13]

He forgives, too: "I assure you, this very day you will be with me in paradise."[14]

He bequeaths: "Mother, this is your son." And to John, "This is your mother."[15]

You are now my child; I am your mother.

He looks at me. Often has he given me his eyes in these thirty years and more, but never has he given them to me more tenderly.

Do not think that his words come easily. Each time he speaks, he must raise himself. He must draw air into his lungs, air to breathe and air to speak. He pushes his pierced wrists and feet against the nails, holds himself erect, renewing the shooting pains, reliving all the agony.

And note that even in his torment, his words, his thoughts, his prayers are first of all for others. Only when he has heard their pleas, spoken and unspoken, does he say, "Why do you abandon me?"[16] and "I am thirsty."[17]

Now, one last time, he draws himself erect. With a great shout, he cries in triumph: "It is now completed."[18] "Father . . . into your hands, I commit my spirit!"[19]

The Sacrifice—the Ransom—the Mass—is over.

And I am glad. I am glad to hold his lifeless body in my arms. He has suffered, never to suffer again.

He has suffered for love of his Father. For him he stretched himself out on the cross. For him he laid down his life: to magnify the Father, to glorify the Father; to win countless souls for his Father.

He has given to God the complete submission of the human will that men refused. He has satisfied divine justice by making exact return of that which man and woman have stolen from the Almighty.

My child, give yourself to him; open your heart to his love; unite your will with his so that in all the world there may be but one will, one love: the will and love of the loving Christ.

◦

Lessons from the Passion

> Rejoice . . . that you share in the sufferings of
> Christ. . . .
>
> 1 PETER 4:13

My other self, I would have you learn three lessons from my passion and death.

The first lesson is the horror and tragedy of sin. It was sin that brought into the world the brutality, the torture, the savagery, the hate which reached their culmination in my crucifixion. Sin unshackled evil. Sin unleashed death.

You, like all men, have the awful power to withhold your will from me. How would you feel if the person dearest to you in all the earth should deliberately turn away from you to choose a life of utmost misery? That is how I feel when a soul rejects me, choosing misery in preference to happiness so complete and rich it never entered the mind of man to conceive of it.

It is then that I say as I said of Jerusalem: "How often have I been willing to gather your children as a mother bird gathers her brood under her wings! But you refused it!"[20]

The second lesson is how to conform your life to the divine will in the midst of sin. My Father wills that men should be free. Though men's freedom perverted by sin led to my bitter suffering, I accepted it. Adam refused to conform to the divine will in a matter that cost him only his pride. The Son of Man conformed to the divine will in a matter that cost him his life. So you must do. Never curse your God, my other self, for what men's sins do to you.

My executioners crucified me by misusing the power I gave them. I, myself, enabled them to strike with the hammer. Of themselves they could do nothing. Does not this give you new insight into the humility with which you should accept the Father's will and the abandonment with which you should seek to carry out the tasks he gives you?

The third lesson is that you can endure anything sin can hurl against you if only you throw yourself trustingly upon me. That is how the saints were able to accept martyrdom. That is how you, too, will be able to accept martyrdom, if this should be the divine will for you.

Suffering is necessary to bring the mind and body into subjection. Either you will be the slave of your passions or you will be their master. Rightly endured, suffering will help make you free. I gave you example by suffering every torment imaginable; torture in every limb, every joint; torture in my back and head; mental agony of anticipation, knowing the torment that was to come, knowing the day and the hour; mental agony of sorrow at the betrayal of my onetime comrade; mental agony of revulsion as I was spat upon; mental agony of shame as I was exposed to obscenity; mental agony of dereliction as I was abandoned on the cross; mental agony to the utmost as I watched my Mother's own martyrdom.

Every sorrow was mine, my other self. As I conquered them all, so I promise you that you also can conquer whatever suffering I ask of you; yes, conquer and rise again with new control over your passions and something regained of the integrity humankind lost through the first human sin.

Learn these lessons. And know this as well.

Though my soul was sorrowful beyond measure, even to the extent of asking my Father to let this chalice pass from me, yet I had one sweet consolation: the thought of my Mother, my saints, and you. You would understand me; you would be loyal to me; you would love me so much the more because these others hated me; you would follow me so much the more closely because my disciples left me; you would watch and pray so much the longer because my chosen three slept in the garden. You would come to me more often in the Sacrament of my love; you would live for me and in me; you would be, with me, the Father's victim; you would join your life to my Calvary in one gloriously redemptive and atoning Mass.

Thus, my other self, I was consoled.

Knowing this, can you fail me? Can you ever, with full deliberation, sin again?

chapter nine

THE MASS AND THE EUCHARIST

The Mass

> Christ . . . delivered himself for us as an
> offering to God. . . .
>
> EPHESIANS 5:2

Before Gethsemani's agony, I said to my Father, "I do not pray for them alone [my Apostles]; I also pray for those who through their preaching will believe in me."[1] I was thinking of you.

Again, on the cross, I prayed, "Father, forgive them," and you were in my mind.

I think of you still and pray for you in exactly this same way in every Sacrifice of the Mass.

Your God prays for *you!*

What more have you to desire?

The Mass, my other self, is the perfect act of worship. Before I came to earth no man, no woman, not even my own Mother, could give to the Trinity a perfect worship. Now you can send aloft perfect homage every time the Mass is offered.

What is this perfect worship? It is the renewal of my sacrifice on Calvary. Go back to what I have told you of my Passion. Relive my agony in Gethsemani; recall the utter contempt with which my creatures spat in my face; let your flesh quiver under the cruel whips and your head weep copious blood through a hundred thorn-torn wounds; carry the ponderous beam through the jeering hordes; let yourself be nailed to it and hang there until merciful death stills your every pain.

This is the Mass.

Yet the Mass is far more. Other men had been crucified. Their crosses were not altars from which rose perfect worship. Their deaths were not the Mass.

The Mass is more than suffering. Its essence is the union of the human will of the God-man with the divine will of his Father. Had I hung upon the tree forever without the free offering of my will, there would have been no perfect homage, no salvation for mankind, no Mass.

The Mass is the offering to my Father of my whole will, even unto death. It is the giving of my entire life, with the cross as its culmination. Calvary was the supreme act of sacrifice because of the torment I endured, because of the love with which I embraced it, and because the Person who offered it was God himself. This offering of love, this supreme worship, I renew in an unbloody manner every time the Mass is offered.

Do you now begin to see a little more clearly how the Mass glorifies God in a perfect way? I, myself, through the priest, give to my Father from the altar the very same adoration, reparation, thanksgiving, petition, and love that I gave him on the cross.

I abandon myself wholly to his will. Since, as man, I am the summit of creation, the highest of all creatures, humanity introduced into the Trinity itself, and since I unite my will completely to his, I give perfect testimony that God is the Supreme Ruler and that all creation depends absolutely upon him. This is adoration.

I yield myself in atonement for all the faults of humanity. By my total submission to my Father's direct and permissive will, submission not only to what he decrees must happen but to all that he permits to occur, I make up for all the rebellions of men. This is reparation.

I give myself in praise to my Father as the munificent Benefactor of all men, and this praise that I offer is equal to all the gifts he has bestowed. This is thanksgiving.

I offer myself in petition, saying once again, "Father, forgive them; and not only forgive them, but pour out upon them a flood of grace so that they may be truly sorry for their offenses and their sins may be washed away and their souls become white as snow." I beg for you! I demand that my Father accept my offering as your offering. My body as your body, my blood as your blood, my whole will as your whole will, that my atonement, my adoration, my praise, my petition, my love may be applied to you as though they were your own.

My mouth on the cross and in the Mass becomes your mouth, and through it you praise the Father.

My hands, pierced by nails, become your hands, and through them you serve the Father. My feet, transfixed to the cross, become your feet, and with them you walk in the ways of the Father. My heart, laid open with a lance, becomes your heart, and through it you silently pour forth your love for the Father. My thoughts, centered always on my Father, become your thoughts, and through them you give to the Father nothing less than your all.

You share in my Mass, my other self. You share also in my work.

Just as I carried on my shoulders not only the cross but the sins of all the world, so you, to the extent I permit you, carry the sins of all mankind, past, present, and to come.

You, too, have power to purchase men's salvation.

You, also, are charged with the ransoming of souls.

You adore for those who do not adore, for those who adore seldom, for those who adore indifferently. You render thanks for all these others; thanks and love and petition and reparation.

How much depends on you! How many sinners, unbelievers, scoffers, indifferent souls need the grace of your Masses! How many souls in purgatory call to you for help! In your hands is the means to provide spiritual strength for all my Church. Though you yourself are spiritually penniless, all that I possess is yours. One Mass, devoutly offered, in complete and perfect union with my will, can do more than enough.

Such a Mass does more to achieve peace and happiness on earth than all the conferences of all world leaders since time began.

Love the Mass, my other self, for it is the Mass that brings salvation to the world.

Offering the Mass

> Holy, Holy, Holy, Lord God of hosts.
>
> Isaiah 6:3

You wish to know how you can best join me in offering this perfect worship.

First, join your intention to that of my Church by willing every day to participate in all Masses everywhere. Second, offer the Mass as often as your circumstances permit.

Offer your Mass as closely as possible in union with the priest. Realize what you do. Imitate the Victim you offer. Let my dispositions be your dispositions. Be humble. Be trusting. Be loving.

The first parts of the Mass, the *Confiteor* and *Kyrie,* express your sorrow for sin.

The *Gloria* gives you opportunity to adore, thank, and bless the Trinity.

At the *Collects* you petition for the aid you need to live my life.

During the *Epistle, Gospel,* and *Credo* you renew your faith.

With this preparation you are ready for the happy, solemn moment that is the *Offertory.* The priest prays, "Accept, O holy Father, almighty and eternal God, this spotless host . . ." and he lifts heavenward the little gold plate on which the host rests. This round, white wafer, so weightless, so unimposing, represents me; it will soon become me.

Do you realize that it represents you also?

A moment later the priest pours wine into the chalice and adds just a drop of water. "O God," he prays, "grant that through the mystery of this water and wine, we may be made partakers of his divinity, who has deigned to partake of our humanity, Jesus Christ. . . ." And the water mingles with the wine. How do you partake of my divinity? Through the union of your will with mine. Let this drop of water signify your will, intermingling with the wine of my will, dissolving in my will, becoming inseparable from my will, so that all that you do becomes mine and all that I do becomes yours.

Give yourself to the Father, even as I give myself to him. Make a conscious surrender of your entire being.

Place on the little gold plate your willing acceptance of all that is joyous in your life and all that is painful, past, present, and yet to come. Perhaps something bitter happened to you yesterday; put it on the plate. Surely something recently made you glad; put it on the plate. Hold nothing back. Offer your all.

Having given yourself, you again render thanks in the *Preface of the Mass.* This is quickly followed by the *Canon* as you prepare for the stupendous miracle of love that is shortly to take place.

In the Canon of the Mass, you join in prayer with the angels and saints, with my Mother, and above all with me. You beg peace and unity for my Church. You implore all that is good for the souls of those present and for those dear to you. And there falls over the church a deep silence. In expectancy of the miracle, the world itself seems almost to have stopped breathing. During this silence renounce yourself anew. Lose yourself in me as the drop of water has lost itself in the wine. Desire nothing but what I desire.

And now, the all-conquering, timeless moment. The priest, good or bad as he may be, performs a miracle greater by far than my raising of Lazarus.

He speaks my words. At once—I AM THERE. I am there as God. I am there as man. I am there as my Father's Victim. I am there as your food.

This Host held aloft, this Host that the priest and you and I offer together, this Host is myself.

But (would you dare believe this, did I not say it?) because you are my other self, and because you are one with me in my Mystical Body, this host in a mystical but real way is also you.

When the priest raises the chalice of my blood, he holds aloft also your life and your will, for this is the chalice in which a moment ago a drop of water intermingled with wine and became my saving blood.

By the action of your will, your life has been dipped into the chalice of my Blood. It is now an offering your God cannot resist, for how can my Father resist me? Because your life is mystically intermingled with mine in the chalice, you have the right, so to speak, to place your finger on the lip of the cup and tip it a little so that a drop of the all-cleansing blood may fall upon the sins of men and wipe them away as though they had never been: your sins, my other self, and those of your family and friends, yes, the sins of your parish, your community, your nation, the whole world.

At this moment how your soul is flooded with grace! Thenceforth you are capable of doing all that you need do to achieve perfection. You have unlocked the door to my Father's treasure house. Your mind is enlightened and your will strengthened; you are persuaded and attracted to do my will in all things. You are given courage and perseverance. Part at least of the temporal punishment due to your sins, for which you are sorry (and how could you help but be sorry for all of them?) is satisfied. And not only is this true of your sins but it is true also of the temporal punishment due to the sins of others, both living and dead.

You know that the Mass would be lacking if the priest stopped after the Consecration. He must complete it. So, too, your Mass is incomplete unless you live it. In your offering of your joys and sorrows, you consecrated all to me. Now I desire that you continue your offering. Renew it consciously often during the day, when you are pleased, when you are annoyed or disappointed, when you are fatigued or hurt.

This is what makes the Mass different from the cross: your offering of *your self.* And this is what makes today's Mass different from yesterday's: that each day you have something new to offer.

Finally, let your Mass be a preparation for your own great act of sacrifice, your death. Just as throughout my life I offered to my Father the Passion and death that were to come, so you should offer to him all of your sacrifices even to the laying down of your life that is to come.

"It is now completed. Father, into your hands I commit my Spirit."[2] In those words I bound up all the works, thoughts, words, and prayers of my life. I commended all to him. All was achieved, the ransom paid, the captives liberated, heaven opened. As all of my life was packaged in that one act of union, so let it be in your Mass.

Do this, my other self, and you shall surely be satiated with the abundance of my grace. I give you to drink of the torrent of my delights. For I am the fountain of life, flowing continuously in the Mass and the Eucharist.

The Humility of the Eucharist

> Verily, thou art a hidden God.
>
> ISAIAH 45:15

In an earlier conversation I told you that, had you been at the Last Supper, you would have learned two lessons: love and humility.

When you begin to understand the Eucharist, my other self, you will begin to comprehend the depths of my love for you, and the extent of my humility. Look at the Host, this small, round, flat disk having the appearance of a wafer of bread. Never were appearances so deceiving!

This seeming host is man, myself, Jesus Christ, born of the Holy Spirit and Mary, healer of lepers, giver of sight. It is he who wept at Lazarus' grave, who asked drink of the Samaritan woman, who whipped the money-changers, who forgave the adulteress; it is Jesus, the Healer, the Teacher, the Savior. This Host is man—myself.

But more wonderful by far, this Host is God: all-mighty, all-knowing, all-holy, all-good, all-loving. This seeming bread is the Will who brought all things out of nothingness, the Power who keeps the universe in existence, the Intelligence from whom all knowledge and order spring.

This Host is the God of whom thousands of years ago the psalmist sang: "Thou hast spread out the heavens like a curtain. . . ."[3]

This Host made you, keeps you in existence, else you would not only die, you would be annihilated so that nothing whatsoever would remain, not even your spirit.

This Host provides your food and shelter, sends you all your good thoughts and impulses.

This Host will one day judge you.

This Host is God—and man—myself. You say it, but you cannot comprehend it. And this Host loves you so dearly that It calls you to be Its other self. It has planned your road, has made Itself the very food of your soul so that you may partake in a wondrous intimacy of Its own nature.

Look at the Host, knowing that you gaze at one real Person with two natures: the nature of God and the nature of man.

Because I am man, you can love me as you love other human beings. You owe me this love, the kind of love my Apostles gave me before they knew me as God, and the love they had for my humanity after they recognized my Divinity. I welcome this love of human for human.

But you owe me also the love of a creature for its God: the love of adoration, the love of complete self-surrender and absolute union with my will.

I trust myself to you in the Eucharist. Trust yourself also to me!

Do you sometimes try to puzzle out how I can be present in the Eucharist? How can it be that this wafer of bread suddenly is bread no more, but the God-man?

Do you ever try to understand how bread and meat and drink become your body and blood? You eat and I do the rest. If I change bread into your body, why should

I find it more difficult to change bread into my body? Do you think it is harder because it is instantaneous rather than gradual? There is no time with God. An instant lasts forever, and forever is but an instant. Does it help you to understand if you think of it like this: I have all eternity to change this bread into myself?

But you ask: "Why, Lord? Why do you do this?" You are thinking perhaps of those who were revolted because I said they must eat my body and drink my Blood.

Yet who is revolted when one human being gives his blood to another? You give your blood in transfusion to be the physical source of mortal life for your fellow men. I give my blood, in an unbloody manner, to be the source of your immortal life.

Who is revolted when a mother feeds a baby with the milk of her breasts? See how I repay men a thousandfold for whatever love they show me. Mary gave to me of herself, and because she is the mother of mankind I give men my whole self. Mary fed me at her breast. I feed you with my very Self within your breast, within your soul.

Can you think of a better way for me to give you spiritual sustenance? Is there a more efficacious method of helping you become my other self?

Do you not see the love that prompts your God? How zealously I work to bring you close to me.

Because I was so far off that you could not grasp me, I became one of you, a man even as you, a creature that you could throw your arms around. Then, indeed, men grasped me, grasped me and crucified me.

Even this was too little. Because I wanted to be still closer to you, closer indeed than I was as your brother man, I delved deep into the depths of my divine wisdom and love and I decided to give you my very Self.

But how? I had made myself man like unto you so you could grasp God's love. Now in order to give myself to you so completely as was my desire, I had to make myself *unlike* you. I hid myself under the likeness of commonplace foods, because I did not want you to shrink from coming to me.

Your God will not rest until he has brought you close to himself! He reveals and he conceals. He comes close and goes afar. He makes himself plain and he makes himself mysterious. He becomes man and he becomes as bread, whatever is easier for you, better for you, best adapted to serve your weakness.

I make myself into whatever you need, as though you were the lord, and I were your servant.

The Love of the Eucharist

Behold, I am here.

ISAIAH 52:6

Look at a tiny, helpless baby. I was such an infant once! But I am more helpless still in the Host.

With Godlike steps I descended: from heaven to Mary's womb, from her womb to a manger, from the manger to a cross, from the cross to a morsel of bread and a cup of wine; so that by becoming your food I might transform you into me, and with Godlike steps we might ascend, through the cross, through the manger of detachment from selfishness, through the motherhood of Mary, to the heaven of the Blessed Trinity.

For nine months I was imprisoned within a creature's body, yet not merely as you were imprisoned within your mother when you were an unborn baby. You had no sense of limitation. But the God-man who dwelt within Mary had, then and there, a mind more intelligent by far than any other human could ever possess. Humanly, I could crave freedom even as you would have.

I am even more dependent, even more closely imprisoned, in the Holy Eucharist.

Mary bore me within herself; so do you. Mary lifted me in her arms; you lift me on your tongue. Are you reverent as Mary was? Do you gaze on me lovingly as Mary did? Do you speak with me, listen to me, and spiritually fall at my feet, confessing your nothingness, as Mary did?

You can receive me often or never, worthily or unworthily, reverently or with indifference; I am waiting early in the day and late. If you ask me, I will come to you spiritually whenever you cannot receive me bodily. I yearn to unite myself with you in the closest union possible. I come to you as man; I come to you as God—and all for love.

All this I thought of when I took bread and raising my eyes to heaven, to my Almighty Father, gave thanks, and said: "This is my body!"[4]

It was not a mere gesture, this raising of my eyes to my Father. I have told you that I instituted the Eucharist for love. It was for love of you, but mostly it was for love of my Father. This was his will. And do you not see that it was, in a sense, a greater sacrifice to give myself in this way to be the food of mankind than to die on the cross? Actually it was the same sacrifice. But think now. Would it not be easier for you once to die than for all time to give your body and soul into the hands of men? To be their food? To be desecrated by some? To be ignored by most?

You would not give even your picture to men, all men, to use as they saw fit so long as time should last, much less your living body and soul.

So I say to you that I gave myself in the Eucharist more completely, if possible, than I gave myself on the cross; I delivered myself in the Eucharist more fully *to* you than I did on the cross *for* you.

How intimate is this union of selves to which I call you in the Blessed Eucharist?

Let us see.

The union of husband and wife in a good marriage is a fusion of two bodies, two souls, two lives. Is our union in the Blessed Eucharist as intimate?

It is more intimate by far!

The union of a mother and the child in her womb unites two bodies in one. The child is flesh of its mother's flesh and bone of her bone. When you receive me in Holy Communion, I am within you, body and blood, soul and divinity, just as truly as the unborn babe is within its mother. Ordinarily you do not feel my presence (though if it is best for you, I will give you even this immense consolation and grace). Yet I am united to you immeasurably more intimately than are the babe and its mother.

The union of your soul with your body makes you a person. Can you conceive of a more complete union than this?

Yet our union in the Sacrament is more complete still.

Almost can I say, though this is but an analogy, that the Eucharist unites us as the Incarnation united my two natures, yes, as my sacred humanity is joined to the eternal sonship.

Do these thoughts strike fire within you? With all my heart, I want to show you what the Eucharist is, what it means, what it does.

Must I give you further analogies?

As melted wax intermingles with melted wax, as flames of fire intermingle with other flames of fire, as cream and sugar are assimilated into every drop of a cup of coffee, as sea water intermingles with fresh water, so we intermingle, you and I, when I come to you in the Eucharist. I am nearer to your soul than your soul is to itself. I am *in* you! You are in me! In Baptism you were made part of my Mystical Body. But now in the Eucharist, we become one flesh. We have, in a sense, the same body, the same blood. Give yourself over to me wholly and we shall have, sooner than you think, the same affections, the same desires, the same will.

Co-operation with Christ

I am the bread of Life.

JOHN 6:35

The fruits of the Eucharist depend in part on your disposition and co-operation with me.

Our union is closer and more fruitful according to how fully you return my love and heed the promptings of the Holy Spirit. Just as the patient who co-operates fully with his doctor has a better response to treatment than if he responded indifferently, so it is with you.

Our union can be as close and as lasting as you choose to make it.

Let all your actions, thoughts, and desires help prepare you. Do all your daily duties as perfectly as you can, with the pure intention of serving me. Thus you will be able to say as I did: "I do always the things that please him."

Strive to realize your unworthiness. Who are you that your God should come to you at all, much less as your food? Who are you that the Eternal Reality—HE WHO IS!—should unite himself with you in a union whose intimacy you can hardly begin to comprehend?

Thinking thus, you will be stimulated to desire to receive me. Feed your desire with acts of love. Blow on the sparks, so to speak, to fan them into leaping flames. Many of my saints longed for Holy Communion day and night. Such desire is not beyond you. Behold I stand at the gate and knock. If any man shall hear my voice, and open to me the door, I will come into him and will sup with him and he with me. Open to me the door of your heart, my other self.

Does this mean that you must come to me with burning emotion, heaving breast, and wild eye? No, come calmly, serenely, peacefully. Offer your will, your understanding, your memory, your body, your soul. Offer me your inability to pray as you would like to pray.

As I am borne along the rail by the priest, making my way to you, cry out in your heart, "Son of David, have mercy on me!" Speak to me, with or without words according as I move you, in acts of faith, hope, love. Beg my Mother to help you receive me as you should; She is beside you as I come to you. Beseech my Father and the Holy Spirit to prepare within you a fitting habitation for me.

When you receive me, offer to my Father the same limitless love with which I died to do his will. Give yourself to me so that I may offer you to the Father in recompense, thanksgiving, petition, and love.

Speak to me in such sentiments as these:

> O Lord, who comes to dwell bodily in my soul
> and who remains with me spiritually all the days
> and nights of my life, help me to build for you,
> your Father and the Holy Spirit a more fitting
> habitation than I can now offer you. Bid St.
> Joseph, your foster father, to help teach me this
> carpentry of the soul. Ask your Mother to direct
> the decoration and arrangement of your home in
> my soul even as she did in Nazareth. Let your

> choirs of angels make music for you and your
> hosts of angels and saints wait upon you and
> engage you in the heavenly conversation of love.
>
> Light up this your Home with the light of faith.
> Make it comfortable with the furnishings of trust.
> Warm it with the fire of love. Strengthen its foun-
> dations with humility and patience.
>
> And, O Lord, allow me, your weak and unworthy
> servant, whom you have made your brother, and
> with you the son and heir of the King of All, to
> wait upon your desires, to serve you and love you
> from the depths of my soul as is fitting for your
> divine nature.

Have faith. Beg me for faith. I cannot refuse you. Petition me for the faith of a Louis of France. Do you know that one day members of his household came to him in fevered excitement, telling him that I had revealed myself in the Blessed Sacrament, and urging him to come quickly to see the Lord? But Louis, prompted by the Holy Spirit, replied that he had no need to see me with his eyes. He knew that I was present; he preferred to be one of those blessed ones who have not seen and yet have believed.

Is such faith beyond you? Not if you desire it as Louis desired.

Have faith! and well might you say with Catherine of Siena:

O Trinity! Eternal Trinity! O Fire, O Abyss of Love!
Would it not have sufficed to create us after your
own image and likeness, making us reborn
through grace, by the Blood of your Son? Was it still
necessary that you should give the Holy Trinity
itself as food for our souls? Yet your love willed
this, O Eternal Trinity! You gave us not only your
Word through the Redemption and in the
Eucharist, but yourself in your fullness of love for
your creature. In very truth the soul possesses you
who are Supreme Goodness.[5]

Christ Lives in the Communicant

He who eats this bread will live forever.

JOHN 6:58

As my humanity is the fruit of a wedding between
God and woman, the love of God for Mary and the love
of Mary for God, so also within you the love of your
God for you and your love for him is to result in the
birth of a new Christ. You are to be transformed into
me through the Eucharist.

Just as truly as a sculptor works on marble or stone,
chiseling out the likeness of his design, I work on your
soul, only so much more quietly, effectively, fruitfully.
Unknown to you, often unseen by your closest friends,
my features emerge. Human eyes may not see them,
but my Father sees, is pleased, showers his grace upon
you, and enfolds you in his love.

Sometimes, often when you least expect it, I give
you evidence of my transforming action. You get up in

the morning and perhaps you are cross and still crave sleep. You find everything going wrong as you dress. You come to Mass and you are so full of distractions that prayer is well-nigh impossible.

And then suddenly you realize that I am on the altar, that I am truly the Host, that what looks like wine is truly my blood that was shed for you. You *know* I am there. You could not know it more if you saw me with your eyes.

With all your heart you speak to me, yet you say not a word; you adore me, yet you do nothing; you thank me, yet you are motionless and passive.

YOU RECEIVE ME!

Then, in your speechless adoration, thanks, and love, you begin to understand what Paul meant when he wrote: "It is now no longer I who live, but Christ lives in me."[6]

My presence interpenetrates your entire being. You have become, in a sense, only a shell. It is I who rule you. We have but one heart, one mind, one will. Guiding, directing, or inspiring you, I take over the course of your life. I discipline you; your imagination, memory, understanding, and your will to make them harmonize with mine. I mold your thoughts, your desires, your standards. I cause you to love not God's gifts but God himself.

You refer everything to me. My will, not yours, is your guiding principle. You abdicate your own will, and seek only mine.

When I live in you thus then you are indeed my other self! Then indeed you desire naught but what I send and refuse naught that I confer or permit. Your life is wholly in my hands. There you have placed it, there you desire it to be.

With your Christ living in you, you give to the three Persons of the Trinity the glory that is Their due: adoration, thanksgiving, love such as your Maker, your Savior, your Sanctifier, deserve.

Yet you do not know the wonders that are taking place within your soul. In the Eucharist I do not come to you alone. Where I am, there is my Father also; and where we are, the Father and I, there the Holy Spirit must also be.

And where we are, Father, Son, and Holy Spirit, there is heaven.

In his ceaseless activity the Father utters the Word, the Son, myself; and the Father and I mutually express our Love; and that Love is the Holy Spirit.

This is what takes place in your soul, this activity of the Trinity, this foretaste of heaven. You do not possess Us, seeing Us face to face as do the saints of the Church Triumphant, but you can possess Us as far as is possible by faith.

If only your faith were perfect, Holy Communion would be for you almost heaven. Indeed, for some of my saints Holy Communion has been an almost-heaven, even while they were still on earth.

During some 10 to 15 minutes after you receive me, for as long as the Host retains the characteristics of bread, I am sacramentally present within you. I bring you a tremendous outpouring of grace, filling your soul with life and strength. I cleanse your soul of every venial sin for which you are sorry and for which you retain no affection. I make your soul strong against temptation. How could it be otherwise when I live in you!

But what happens then? Do I leave you until tomorrow? No! True, after these precious moments of sacramental union, my body, blood, and soul are no longer within you. Yet we are still bound in a union that is wondrously close. My divinity remains with you and within you. The Holy Spirit who dwells within my own human soul stays with you in a special way. Within your soul, he incites thoughts, desires, and dispositions that are similar to the thoughts, desires, and dispositions of my own soul.

The Father, the Holy Spirit, and I continue to live in you; We *abide* in you. Almost as We three indwell in one another, so We indwell in you. You have fellowship with the Father, and with his Son, Jesus Christ. Your soul is a heaven, for God himself dwells there.

And so it is—wondrous truth!—that when you leave the church and go about the business of the day, We three abide in you in this special spiritual way.

You walk with the Trinity; you possess *Life* itself. As my activities never lessened my contemplation, so it should be with you.

In the service of your family, your employer, your clients; in your dealings with your employees, your inferiors, your children; in your relations with your friends, your acquaintances, your neighbors: remember your GOD DWELLS WITHIN YOU—YOU ARE IN A SPECIAL WAY MY OTHER SELF!

You work, not you alone, but I work in you.

You serve others, and it is not you alone that serve, but I serve in you.

You suffer, not you alone, but I suffer in you.

You laugh, not you alone, but I laugh in you.

You are a victim with me; you adore with me; you give thanks with me; you love with me. You live now, not yourself alone, but I live in you! You are my other self.

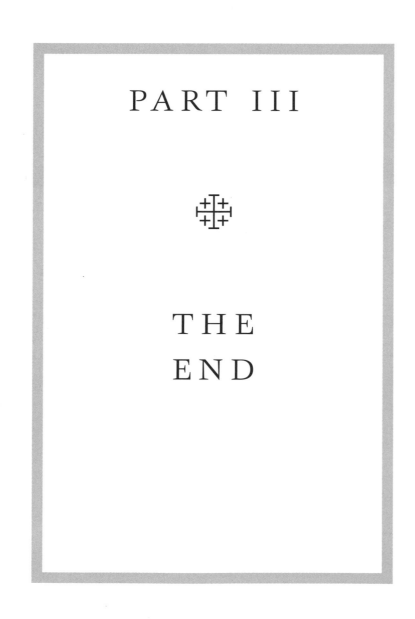

PART III

THE
END

chapter ten

THE FINAL GOAL

A Witness for Christ

> You are the witnesses. . . .
>
> Luke 24:48

Now it is time to sum up.

If you would be truly my other self, you must carry on my work. My task is to bring all men into my Mystical Body. You are to help.

Just before I ascended to my Father, I told my Apostles: ". . . you shall be my witnesses in Jerusalem and in all Judea and Samaria and even to the very ends of the earth."[1]

You also, my other self, are to be my witness.

What kind of witness are you?

When your religion is attacked or misrepresented in conversation, are you silent? When a filthy story is told, do you approve it by hearty laughter? When my name is profaned, are you afraid to show your displeasure?

Perhaps you rationalize your timidity. If I show my displeasure, you tell yourself, I shall make myself unpopular and less effective in promoting the "positive" aspects of the Faith.

Peter and John were brought before the rulers, elders, and scribes, and warned to teach no more in my name. Here was their answer: "Whether it is right in the sight of God to listen to you rather than to God, decide for yourselves. We cannot refrain from speaking of what we have seen and heard."[2]

Stephen, the first of all my followers to die for the Faith, boldly stood up before the Council and recited the whole history of persecution of the prophets. He accused the Council of resisting the Holy Spirit just as their fathers had done. Carried away by fury, they stoned him.

Paul approached anyone, Jew, Gentile, governor, magician, learned men of Athens, as well as the multitudes. In the markets and parks, in synagogues and private homes, he preached fervently in my name, striking up conversation with one person or dozens, always introducing the good news of man's salvation and God's love.

I do not say that you are called to preach as Peter, Stephen, and Paul. But in ways that accord with your state in life, you are to be my witness.

I promise you as I did Paul, "Do not fear, but speak. Do not be silent, because I am with you and no one shall lay a hand on you to harm you."[3] Be doubtful and afraid no longer. Look no more for excuses, for modifications, for easy ways to be my witness. You have my pledge; let it be enough.

Your doubts are born of pride. They are founded on the notion that your success depends on you. No wonder you temporize!

You have only to supply the good will to serve me and I will bulwark your mind and body with my own strength. With my help, you can, and you will, be my witness. Though you may still have a natural reluctance to be "queer" in others' eyes, do not hesitate. Throw yourself upon me. Speak your mind quietly. Give me your good will and I will give you words, strength, courage.

I do not say that you can be my apostle without effort. Do not think that Paul had only to enter a city, preach a sermon or two, baptize the converts who flocked to him by the thousands, and then go on his way to new fields and new cities.

Paul preached for many years in the regions of Syria and Cilicia. He was in Antioch for a year, in Corinth for eighteen months, in Ephesus for three years. He taught now here, now there, staying where he was well received, leaving when he was too long unheard or abused or tormented. He taught for three months in the synagogue at Ephesus; then, because of violent and long-continued disputes there, he withdrew to the school of a certain Tyrannus and there he taught daily for two years.

Paul made prodigious efforts and met with violent opposition, far more than you will be called upon to withstand. But he was so zealous that even when he was a prisoner in Rome he called men to him to teach them. This he did for two years, while also finding time and energy to write many of his letters.

No, I do not promise to spare you work and trials; but I will make your burden light. Carry only a sliver of my cross, and I will carry all except a sliver of yours.

You will meet with rebuffs as I did when I foretold the Eucharist. It was too hard a saying. You may have to endure calumny, false charges, scandals, as I endured the charge that I had a devil.

Your friends and relatives may turn against you and wound you, as I was wounded when my relatives thought me beside myself.

Yet all the while I will be with you. Deep within your soul I will give you consolation that your sufferings are not worthy to be compared with the delight of being my witness.

A Witness by Example

> So let your light shine before your fellow men. . . .
> MATTHEW 5:16

I ask you gently to correct clear and manifest wrongdoing that falls within your province, but I warn you most seriously against becoming a faultfinder. In all things be charitable, whenever possible putting a good interpretation on others' words and actions. Others act somewhat as they think you expect them to act. A double-meaning remark is often completely disarmed when you, in the spirit of charity, react as though it were entirely innocent.

Beware of being a spoilsport or of looking for evil.

Be careful not to "preach." In conversation neither avoid religion nor intrude it artificially. Be natural and reasonable.

Above all, be my witness by your example. The witness of your manner and actions, either for or against me, is immeasurably more powerful than that of your words.

In a reasonable way strive to make and keep yourself attractive. Be neat in dress, kindly in manner, charitable in speech, helpful in action. Do your work diligently. Use the things of the world wisely, for my sake, so that others will think well of you and your influence among them may be more effective.

Be zealous. So many of your fellow men know little or nothing about me. So many members of my Church think of me seldom. Show by your example what it is to be my other self.

By your frequent presence, daily if possible, show how much the Mass and Holy Communion mean to you.

Show how much you value prayer. Visit me frequently in church. Participate in Rosary devotions and seek my Benediction.

According to your ability, your time, and your station, take part in parish activities. There are many such ways to be my witness: through the Holy Name Society, the Sodality, the Legion of Mary, the St. Vincent de Paul Society, the Nocturnal Adoration Society, mothers' clubs, the Cana Movement, the Christian Family Movement, and others. Though you cannot belong to all of these organizations, you should certainly belong to some of them.

Being my other self should make you different in a wholesome, attractive, holy way. At home, in your work, in recreation, wherever you may be, whatever you may do, this difference will bear witness to me.

There should be about you an aura of calm serenity, fitting one who has abandoned his will to that of the all-loving, all-wise, all-powerful God. In an age of unrest, doubt, and fear, you should be a rock of confidence.

Your face should exhibit the gentle strength that is the handiwork and trademark of holiness.

There should be in your manner such an undercurrent of joy and gladness that others will be happy to be with you.

Most important, the atmosphere of charity should envelop you as a mantle. Your actions and attitudes should point quietly to one fact: that you love your neighbor as I love you. Show others that you love them, not in explicit words, except where words are natural and appropriate, but in deeds. Think of others as "Christ." Serve me through them, preaching my Gospel of love by your life. Let your words, voice, manner, and deeds tell the members of my Mystical Body, and potential members as well, that you love them as I love them, enough to die for them, enough to climb the cross on their behalf.

Imitate the spirit of the early Christians who, because they were in the world, did not cut themselves off from all their former observances, but instead persevered in the temple worship and broke bread in this house and that, taking their food gladly, praising God and winning favor with the people.

A Priestly Witness

> Go, therefore, and make all nations your disciples.
>
> MATTHEW 27:19

Peter rightly called the members of my Church "a holy priesthood."[4] Some, ordained priests by the sacrament of Holy Orders, have sacramental power. But all members, laymen, laywomen, and children, are priests by spiritual union with me.

In reasonable accordance with your state in life, therefore, you and all my priests have a duty to teach my doctrine.

Call to mind the parable of the stern master who distributed talents among his servants to use fruitfully until his return for the reckoning. Is not the servant who took his only talent and buried it like the timid Christian who hides his Christianity, fearing to display or speak of it; a Christian in private but a "good fellow" in public? Fearing to expose himself to possible ridicule, he buries in the ground his talent of Christianity. Venturing nothing, he gains nothing.

Is not such a one rightly called a slothful, unprofitable, and wicked servant?

The kingdom of God is like the mustard seed. From a small beginning it must grow until it fills the earth. I need you to speed its growth. I have plans for you in this apostolate.

All about you are neighbors who admit that the Almighty God exists, and little more. They do not know how much I love them. Rarely do they ask themselves: "What does God want me to do in this specific action?" Seldom do they make an effort to discover my will. In the same vague, unrealistic way that they recognize the fact of starvation in China, they recognize the kingdom of God.

This is the great evil of the modern world. The kingdom of God is at hand, but so few accept my rule. They have not fitted it into their lives.

You must help me go to them, my other self. On the street, in the home, the office, the store, the factory; on the playground, at the beach, on the golf course and tennis court; in the hospital, the university, the nursery school; in the courts and the prisons; in the theaters and libraries, you must help me bring them to myself. You must introduce me by your example, recommend me by your life, sustain me by your prayers.

I must give them eternal life. I must help them become saints. And I need you!

Be zealous! Be alert! Be untiring! Be generous!

On the first Christmas, the shepherds did not fear to tell what they had seen and heard.

In the temple Anna, the prophetess, had only to see me and she began to give praise and to speak of me to all who were awaiting the redemption of Jerusalem.

The Magi came and they did not hesitate to ask openly, "Where is the newborn King of the Jews? It was his star we saw in the East, and we came to offer homage to him."[5]

John the Baptist going into all the region of the Jordan, feared not to preach repentance and preparation for my coming.

And Andrew when he met me that first day was not reluctant to seek out his brother and say to him: "We have found the messias!"[6] And he led him to me.

Have I not revealed myself to you far more clearly than I did to any of these? Why do you not seek out your brother and your neighbor and your friend, and say to them, by your life and example, if not in word: "Come with us! We have found the messias, the Savior, the Lord!"

I performed miracles for Peter, John, Philip, Paul, and my other Apostles to give authority to their words. You know how Peter healed the lame beggar who sat at the temple gate, and the palsied Aeneas at the town of Lydda who for eight years had never left his bed. He raised from death the holy woman Tabitha of Joppa. Such power I gave him that the people used to bring their sick into the street and lay them down there on beds and pallets, hoping that Peter's shadow might fall on them as he walked by and they might be healed.

Paul, too, worked wonders in abundance, using the power of my name. He cured the lame man at Lystra, crippled from birth. The young man, Eutychus, who fell three stories out of a window and was picked up dead, Paul brought back to life. Articles of clothing that had touched Paul's body had only to be applied to the sick and the possessed and forthwith they were cured and cleansed.

Can I not, if necessary, do as much for you? Am I less powerful now than I was then? Do I care less now that men should know the truth and live my life? In my own way I will give authority to your words, even by miracles if need be. Your life, your example, your identification with me, will exert such influence that when men see you they will know you are my disciple; and when they hear you, they will believe. This is my pledge.

What an apostle you ought to be! How unworldly your life, how reverent, thankful, and loving toward your God!

I have called you. You are a chosen one. You are my priest.

Be holy; live beyond reproach. Give all men their due. Modest, humble, loving, not repaying injury with injury, or hard words with hard words, but sharing with others the gifts you have received from me, be ready at all times to give an account of your Faith as befits my priest.

Thus you will proclaim the goodness of your God who has called you out of darkness into light, called you to be his witness, called you to be his priest.

A Priestly Victim

> Behold, I am in your hands.
> JEREMIAH 26:14

As my priestly witness you are to teach with me; as my priestly victim you are to offer sacrifice with me.

Every member of my Body is duty-bound to offer sacrifice for sin. You are to help fill in, as Paul said, what is lacking in my own sufferings. Not that my atonement is ineffective, or that one drop of my blood would not suffice to redeem the whole world. On the contrary, I offered far more to the Father than was needed to redeem the human race. This is true because of the complete love with which I suffered; because of the perfection of the life I offered, since it was the life of One who was both God and man; and because of the terrible pain and grief I endured.

Yet something was lacking; your sharing in my atonement through the union of your will with mine.

Give me your perfect willingness to obey and to suffer in union with me. Then nothing is lacking. Never fear, my other self, that I will try you too severely. Trust me. Lean on me. I want to help you even more than you want to be helped.

I have told you that what I did, I did for all the members of my Mystical Body, as though they had done it themselves. I have incorporated you into myself. My life, therefore, is your life; your life is my life. I live in you and you live in me.

It is your priceless privilege to be a victim with me and a coredeemer of mankind. With me, offer your life to the Father. Thus we repair the insults, neglect, and ingratitude of men, past, present, and future.

Offer to the Blessed Trinity every step of your life. Let every moment be a glorification of your God who made you, redeemed you, and who sanctifies you. Let every instant be a "Blessed be God." Offering yourself thus in union with me dwelling within you, you are a holy victim and worthy victim, making right the wrongs of centuries, offering God's own sacrifice to God himself.

Be my victim by abandonment.

As I accepted the word uttered by my Father for my life on earth, so you shall accept God's word for your life.

Give your present and your future completely into my hands. Accept here and now all that my plan for you entails. This is a great sacrifice, but it is also a great joy.

I ask you to do nothing that others have not done before you. Again I would teach you by the example of others.

Zachary and Elizabeth had no children, all their prayers seeming to be unanswered. They had no thought that they should give birth to one of the great figures of history, a son chosen by God to fulfill a key purpose. Yet they went on praying and following all the commandments and observances of the Lord without reproach.

Neither did John the Baptist know what fate awaited him. He understood only that his work of the moment was to preach, baptize, and do penance; and this work he did with all his heart.

Until the Annunciation, Mary did not know what her God had planned for her. But she was the handmaid of the Lord, ready to do his will at all times without hesitation and with full faith.

Joseph knew nothing about Mary's role in the divine plan until the angel revealed it to him.

Peter, the fisherman, never dreamed before I told him that he was destined to be my vicar on earth.

Paul, riding to Damascus to persecute me, had no thought that I should make him my Apostle to the Gentiles.

They knew as little about their future as you know of yours.

They recognize their nothingness, even as I recognized that my human nature was as nothing in relation to the Godhead. Does it not help you to realize your own nothingness when you see this?

If I, as man, was nothing, and so acted, giving my Body over to be scourged and crucified, you also must realize that you are nothing and that your purpose is to complete my plan for you.

Here and now, accept all that will happen to you as the gift of my love. Look upon every day, indeed every moment, as a "grab bag" given to you by One who loves you beyond the power of your mind to conceive. It is full of surprises, of good things, of "treasure." Accept it all.

Give to my Father the perfect obedience that so many men refuse. Be my victim by abandonment.

Victims Winning Victory Over Sin

> Help bear one another's burdens. . . .
>
> Galatians 6:2

Be with me a victim by your prayers.

My Little Flower of Lisieux was confined to her cloister. Yet through her prayers she was not only a great missionary but an effective victim for many.

Catherine of Siena took on herself the sins and sufferings of other souls, making herself victim for them, refusing to cease her prayer and mortification until she had won the victory.

Monica by her prayers did much to win the grace of conversion for Augustine.

While you are on this earth, you will never know the value and the power of prayer.

At the wedding feast in Cana, my Mother's "prayer" changed the timetable of my public life. When I said to her, "My time has not yet come!"[7] I stated a definite fact. It was her request that caused my hour to come then and there.

I also made myself a victim by prayer.

As I prayed for all men, so you must pray for all members of my Mystical Body and for all those outside my fold as well, that all may be one.

Realize that when you pray, you are not only praying as an individual, but as a member of my mystical Body. You are myself praying, and my prayer is perfect. It can convert unbelievers, make saints of sinners, release souls from purgatory, and save the dying from the beckoning flames of hell.

Be with me a victim through prayer.

Be my victim also in pain and in grief. Some suffering and sorrow are the lot of every human, because sin brought pain and grief into the world. But how it saddens me to see the precious gold of suffering thrown aside as though it were useless.

When I said, "Blessed are the sorrowing, for they will be consoled,"[8] I did not speak idly. The priceless blessing I give to those who are most fully my other selves is the ability to turn sorrow into grace.

In your moments of suffering I extend to you my most anxious care and my choicest blessings.

If on the cross, hanging between heaven and the hell that was Calvary, I could give Mary to John and John to Mary, can I forget you in your Gethsemani of grief?

I give you crosses only because they enable you to be a coredeemer of mankind.

You do not know, my other self, how many souls were saved by Mary's sharing in my Passion. This was, in part, why I permitted her to suffer so with me. And this is why I permit you also to suffer with me.

Each sorrow, each pain, each disappointment is a touching of your lips to my cross. These sufferings that I could not bear myself in the short years of my earthly life, I now accept and offer through you. The soldier lying on his hospital bed, leg amputated; the athlete suddenly crippled by polio; the blind, the deaf, and the mute unable to take part in the spontaneous give-and-take of social life; the school boy faced with failure in his examination; the wife or husband unhappily married; the child of a home broken by divorce; the father out of work, being turned away from one office after another: these are sufferings, unborne by me, that I now bear in my other selves, that I now bear in *you*.

Is it not a wonderful privilege thus to supply part of my Passion? Is it not true as Francis de Sales said, "If jealousy could enter into the realm of eternal love, the angels would envy the sufferings of God for man, and those of man for God"?[9]

Give me your suffering.

When illness besets you; when your body cries for rest and your work seems more than you can manage; when the tasks you are called upon to do apparently demean you; when sleeplessness afflicts you, headaches torment you, pangs of hunger assail you:

you are my victim. I join your every pain to my pains of the way of the cross and of Calvary.

When you are tormented by worry that seems beyond your power to control; when you are subjected to ridicule and you lose the respect of others; when you are insulted, passed over, reprimanded; when you quake with fear because of a duty you must perform, a speech you must deliver, a telephone call you must make; when you are helping to take the parish census and not knowing how you will be received; when you must solicit aid or funds; when you suffer the stings of poverty: you are with me a coredeemer. I join all your mental torment to my own dread of the cross when I said to Peter, James, and John, "I am plunged in sorrow. . . ."[10]

When grief assaults you and threatens to overcome you; when your dear ones depart in death's sleep; when dryness and desolation overwhelm you; when temptation charges upon you apparently all-conquering; when you feel that even I have deserted you and your abandoned, broken soul is totally unable to bear another wound, then know this: you are my other self. The more you think you are abandoned, the more I draw you to me. Know that, in this state, there is between me and you the most intimate union. Then you must live by faith alone. Offer me your soul as a victim to do with what I wish.

Then, indeed, your sacrifices are joined to mine. They *are* mine, just as if I had done them myself. And my sacrifices are yours, just as if you had done them yourself.

Then, I make up whatever is lacking in your life, even as you make up what remains to be supplied in my own Passion.

Victims we are; victims we shall be; victim winning victory over sin!

Be My Saint

> You are fellow citizens with the saints. . . .
>
> EPHESIANS 2:19

We are nearing the last of our conversations. I ask you now and for your whole life to be my witness, my victim, my saint.

Yet these conversations must not be our last. Rather, go back again and again over my words. Let not a single day pass without returning to one of our visits, listening carefully, savoring my meaning. So long as you continue to derive benefit from them, let these conversations be the foundation of your daily meditation. Thus at intervals you will renew all that I have told you.

Do this faithfully and you will be, I pledge, my witness, helping me teach my poor bewildered people, my victim, helping me redeem countless souls, my saint, helping me change the world so that it may become the Paradise my Father desires.

Note that I do not say *a* witness but my witness; not *a* victim but my victim; not *a* saint but my saint; yes, not *an*other self but *my* other self.

Do you know what this means? It means that you are unique.

You came into existence through a unique act of my creative love. You continue to live because at every instant I renew this unique act of creative love.

I created you different from everyone else that ever was, is, or will be. Your body is unique. Even the markings of your skin, your fingerprints, set you apart; they are yours alone. If your body is the only one of its precise kind in all the universe, how unique must be your soul.

This is so because I wanted a "you" to exist, you individually; a person who would be uniquely you, the only you that will ever be. I created *you,* and I love *you.*

Have you ever said of two lovers, "I don't know what she sees in him, I don't know what he sees in her"? What one sees in the other is something individual and desirable that others perhaps do not glimpse at all. So it is that your unique characteristics make you individually lovable in my eyes.

In return for my love, I desire the particular and individual love that you and only you can give me.

That is why I tell you to be the person I desire, doing perfectly what is called for by your state in life; in this way you will return the particular and individual love that from all eternity I have wanted from you.

That is why I have told you about the sacrament of the present moment, urging you to offer me every moment in all its circumstances.

Think of it! This very instant is given to you to serve me, and thus to love me, in a particular way that is given no one else in all creation.

Are you sick? Then, at this instant, I want to be loved and served through your unique sickness. Offer it to me. No one else can.

Are you poor? Love and serve me through your poverty. Who but you can offer me this unique gift?

Are you physically handicapped, obscure, brilliant, joyful, sad? Are you struggling with a temptation, a problem, a difficulty? Love me through these ways that I give you.

This is what I see in you: uniqueness, individuality, a capacity for a wholly individual love that you alone can give me and that you alone can receive from me.

I have called you to be my witness, my victim, my saint in a way that no one else ever was, is, or will be.

To every generation my Father gives the saints it needs. Be the saint of his plan. Unite your will with mine, do my work, think my thoughts; in the unique way that is given only to you, be my other self.

Will you do for me what my Mother did in another way centuries ago? Will you give me yourself, so that I may dwell in you, grow in you, and perform the tasks that the Father has placed in the world for us to do?

Your work is to carry out as perfectly as you can your moment-by-moment tasks. If only I can make you see that little things, normal things, are my Father's plan for you, just as for nearly all of my mortal life little and normal things were his plan for me! Oh, that you might have a passion to do his will in little things as I had!

If only I can make you understand that to be a saint is to be a normal human being. My Mother and Joseph and I myself, in all of my human qualities, were like you. We breathed, ate, thought, spoke, walked, played, and prayed as you do.

We worked at making a living, just as did those around us: Joseph and I as carpenters, Peter as a fisherman, Luke as a doctor, Paul as a tentmaker who paid his own way as a missionary and urged others to do likewise.

My saints were as much like you as you are like your neighbors. See your neighbor as he enters his home after the day's work; see the policeman directing traffic at the busy corner; see your grocer, your postman, the members of your immediate family. Are you not as they are in form and stature, in body and mind? Just so, the saints were like you. What they did, you can do also.

Perform your daily tasks as they did theirs. Help me remake the world.

How creation waits for the things that are to come! All creation, said Paul, "awaits with eager longing the manifestation of the sons of God . . . to enjoy the freedom that comes with the glory of the children of God."[11]

To Change the World

Thou shalt fill me with joy with thy countenance.
PSALM 15:11

What a world this would have been had Adam not fallen! No fear of creatures, no pain, no illness, no death. Control over the passions, power fully to enjoy bodily pleasures, but dominance over them, not by them. No need for guns or swords. No H-bombs. The books that would have been written by intellects far keener than Shakespeare's, Dante's, Virgil's. The statues that would have been molded, the buildings constructed, the pictures painted. The love that would have dwelt in this paradise among all men of good will.

Your God made the world, and it was good.

Through sin, evil came into the world, and evil will last so long as sin endures. But it was not so in the beginning, and sin need not enslave men today.

You have read, my other self, of the weakness of my Apostles. They fled when the guards seized me in the garden. But when the Holy Spirit descended upon them on Pentecost, how strong they became! See what happens when the Almighty pours forth his grace in an overwhelming flood to transform weak mortals into my witnesses, my victims, my saints.

There is but one remedy for evil: sanctification. Goodness cannot be legislated; nor can peace, prosperity, and happiness. These are the results of obedience to my law. The state can provide an atmosphere in which such obedience can flourish, but only God can give grace and only individuals can use grace.

Therefore, be my saint. Help me change the world. Aid me to bring peace and joy to all men of good will.

I ardently desire a world free from evil, a world of peace and joy.

I made man for happiness. What is creation, what is sanctification, but a happiness, the one in the natural order, the other in the supernatural, a pouring forth of the divine joy of the Almighty himself?

Sow my peace in your family, in your community. Though the world presents to you a glorification of selfishness and carnality, though it scorns justice and charity, though it scoffs at the thought of working and living for me, you my saint, will stand firm. Nay, more, you will counterattack. You will change the world.

Your counterattack will be joyful. You will show by your own life that happiness is the product of goodness. You will show there is true joy in living as my other self.

Look for joy. Rejoice in the sunlight with which I warm you. Rejoice, as I did, in the green hills of summer, the fresh food of the garden, the cooling rain, the clean air. Rejoice in good books, good thoughts, good friends. Rejoice and be happy in my peace.

Be a *peacemaker,* my other self, a positive force for tranquility, harmony, love.

Do you love all men? The thief who has stolen from you, the gossip who has disparaged you, the competitor who has surpassed you, the slanderer who had slashed your good name? It is much harder to love them than it is to love your faraway "enemies," such as the communist, the radical, the reactionary, the political troublemaker.

If you are truly my other self, you will show your love for all men by doing your best to bring them into my Mystical Body and to make their oneness with me close and lasting.

Bring them to me by cheerfulness, helpfulness, generosity, the spiritual and corporal works of mercy.

All this will sow joy. It will spread my peace through the members of your household, your neighborhood, your community, and these in turn will radiate joy and peace nationwide and worldwide. Whoever you help to become more Christlike will himself sow seeds of joy.

What a life of adventure this is to which I have called you, my saint. The commonplace becomes wonderful, precious, exhilarating. How can a deed be drab that is the price of a human soul, the adoration of the Almighty, the sought-for thanksgiving of the All-Holy!

As my other self, yours is a glory immeasurably greater than the earthly glory of any king. You are mystically identified with me, your God. You are beloved of my Father even as I am beloved of him.

You have only to speak to me, YOUR GOD, and I give you my whole attention.

You have only to act, nay, to think, and you draw without limit on the most precious riches in all existence, riches that ransom souls and remake the world.

As my other self, you reproduce me. What dignity could be more sublime?

Do this, and in my good time the foretaste of heaven you shall enjoy here on earth will be followed by heaven itself. I have destined you for a never ending union with me that is uniquely yours. From all eternity

I foresaw this particular oneness of yourself and myself; and it was good.

You shall have the fullest possession of me that it is possible for you to enjoy. No longer will you know me and love me in a dark, veiled way.

Bathed in the light of the Trinity, you shall have the joy of belonging completely to your God, of being wholly loved by him, of loving him wholly yourself. You shall see infinite Goodness—infinite Beauty—infinite Truth—infinite Love —face to face. You shall know God and knowing him shall love him yet more; and loving him more you shall know him yet better, in an endless chain of knowing and loving that will satisfy all your desires.

This is your destiny: complete happiness in our union, complete joy in your unique possession of your God and his possession of you.

Eye has not seen, nor ear heard, nor has it entered into the heart of man what things your God has prepared for you—for you are my other self —and I am YOUR GOD.

Come, blessed one, prepare to enter into eternal joy!

NOTES

The Priestly Prayer of Jesus Christ

1. John 17:1–11; 14–26.

1. The Goal of Life

1. Psalm 9:2–3.
2. Matthew 6:16.
3. Matthew 11:28.

2. Abandonment

1. Psalm 55:5.
2. Psalm 58:18.
3. John 14:1, 14, 18, 27–28; 15:9.
4. Psalm 130:2, 3.
5. Luke 18:17.
6. Mark 4:40.

3. Be What I Desire

1. Romans 12:6–8, as translated by Ronald Knox in *The New Testament* (New York: Sheed and Ward, Inc., 1948).
2. St. Francis de Sales, *Introduction to the Devout Life*, translated and edited by Rt. Rev. John K. Ryan (New York: Harper and Brothers, 1949), p. 104.
3. St. Francis de Sales, *Treatise on the Love of God*, translated by Henry Benedict Mackey, O.S.B. (Westminster, Md.: The Newman Press, 1944), pp. 362–363.
4. Mark 4:38.

5.   Mark 4:40; Luke 8:25.

6.   Mark 6:35–36.

7.   Matthew 14:16.

8.   John 6:7.

9.   John 6:9.

10. Luke 23:34.

11. Luke 23:43.

4. Christ in Us

1.   Galatians 2:20, Knox translation.

2.   Galatians 3:27–28, Knox translation.

3.   Acts 9:4.

4.   John 17:20–26.

5.   John 14:15; 15:12, 17.

6.   John 13:13–14.

7.   John 18:8.

8.   Luke 23:34.

9.   Luke 23:42–43.

10. Galatians 2:20.

5. Detachment

1.   Matthew 5:29.

2.   Mark 15:30, 32.

3.   Acts 3:6.

4.   Mark 12:43–44.

6. Virtue

1.   John 13:34.

2.   John 3:27.

3.   Matthew 3:15.

4.   Luke 22:42.

5.   2 Corinthians 12:9–10.

6. Litany for Humility, Cardinal Merry del Val.
7. Matthew 5:4.
8. James 1:19–20. Psalm 36:8–9.
9. Psalm 36:8–9. Psalm 36:8–9.

7. *Prayer*

1. John 14:14.
2. Luke 2:48.
3. John 2:3.
4. John 11:3.
5. John 11:21.
6. Letter of St. Francis de Sales to St. Jane de Chantal, quoted in C. F. Kelley, *The Spirit of Love* (New York: Harper and Brothers, 1951), p. 180.
7. *Treatise on the Love of God*, translated by Henry Benedict Mackey, O.S.B. (Westminster, Md.: The Newman Press, 1949), p. 263.
8. John 21:6.

8. *Avoidance of Sin*

1. John 15:5.
2. Mark 14:34.
3. Mark 14:36.
4. Mark 14:37–38.
5. Matthew 26:42.
6. Mark 14:38.
7. Matthew 26:50.
8. Luke 22:48.
9. John 18:4–8.
10. John 18:20, 21.
11. John 19:4, 5.
12. Mark 15:34.

13. Mark 23:34.

14. Luke 23:43.

15. John 19:26, 27.

16. Mark 15:34.

17. John 19:28.

18. John 19:30.

19. Luke 23:46.

20. Luke 13:34.

9. The Mass and the Eucharist

1. John 17:20.

2. John 19:30. Luke 23:46.

3. Psalm 103:2.

4. Luke 22:19.

5. Quoted in *From Holy Communion to the Blessed Trinity*, M. V. Bernadot, O.P., translated by Dom Francis Izard, O.S.B. (Westminster, Md.: The Newman Press, 1948), pp. 24–25.

6. Galatians 2:20.

10. The Final Goal

1. Acts 1:8.

2. Acts 4:19–20.

3. Acts 18:10.

4. 1 Peter 2:5.

5. Matthew 2:2.

6. John 1:41.

7. John 2:4.

8. Matthew 5:5.

9. Quoted in *From Holy Communion to the Blessed Trinity*, M. V. Bernadot, O.P., translated by Dom Francis Izard, O.S.B. (Westminster, Md.: Newman Press, 1948), p. 85.

10. Matthew 26:38.

11. Romans 8:19, 21.